"Reading Get Glowing is almost like being with Ann — only without the perfume. Ann Mincey's optimism and love of life radiates from every page. Each chapter has something to teach us about trying to live our lives better today than yesterday."
— **Brad Moore**
President,
Hallmark Hall of Fame Productions, Inc.

"You've lifted and inspired me yet again. I always enjoy and look forward to your presence but the experience of learning the source of inspiration that gives Ann Mincey the "glow that lights the room" had me feeling as though I was walking in your shoes and hearing your angelic voice. Reading this was like experiencing one of your world famous hugs! You make me glow like no other! Thanks for your abundance of love and inspiration!"
— **Robert Reed**
ERGO Styling Tools

"Ann Mincey draws from the best of what the world's faith traditions offer. She is a compassionate spirit who encourages us to respect and glean from the richness found in all traditions. Ann's life work is a reflection of spiritual truth that transcends all boundaries. She is dedicated to helping salon professionals excel in their craft and bring integrity to their lives and businesses."
— **Laura King**
Interfaith Tapestry Garden
Salon Owner, Style On 2nd
Portland, Oregon

"This book is like a great movie — with the messages lingering long after the story ends. Ann shows us how faith guides us toward living a happy, joyful and successful life. This beautiful, wise and trusted teacher gives us hope for "being a star right where you are."
— **Kathy S. Soverow, M.S., M.Ed.**
Creative Director/CEO
Shape Your Life, Inc.

"GET GLOWING" succeeds as guide book to a more fulfilling life because it has the imprint of authenticity. The principles have been road tested over a lifetime by Ann Mincey herself. Having known Ann since our days in college together, I have watched with admiration as she has consistently applied the philosophy of "GET GLOWING" to her daily life. It has been the source of her strength in both good times bad. The end result is the kind of personal happiness and success we can only envy. Actually we can either envy or we can get busy reading and apply the insights in "GET GLOWING" to our own lives."
— **Boyd Matson**
National Geographic Explorer

"As a life-long friend, confidante, and soul mate, I know Ann has experienced every word in this unique concept that shines new light on life. Read this for YOU!"
— **Martin Parsons**

Ann Mincey

get glowing!

You Are a Star Right Where You Are

Ann Mincey

StarShine Systems
New York, NY

StarShine Systems
235 E. 49th St. 1-H
New York, NY 10017
www.getglowing.com
1-866-445-6946

Special thanks to Authors of Unity

To Christian and Genie for their belief in this work; to Angela Hynes and Cheryl Adam for their mindful and professional editing. Thanks to Jane Mjolsness, Susan Kendrick and Richard Shiro for their valued contribution.

The suggestions in this book for self-development are not meant to substitute the advice of a medical doctor or psychiatrist. It is essential to seek the advice of such a professional in the case of any physical or mental symptoms. The book contains only ideas, practices, and opinions of the author.

ISBN: 0-9764941-0-8

Library of Congress Control Number: 2005900870

To My Families:

My parents, Reverend Wesley and Pauline Poole.
My entire Poole and Bearinger families for preaching
"You are the light of the world."
My REDKEN 5th Avenue NYC and L'Oreal families for teaching
"You are a star right where you are."
My professional beauty industry family and lifelong friends for reaching—
"You are a work of heart!"
And to Martin Parsons—"You are a light, a star, and have my heart."

table of contents

the genesis of *get glowing*

"Be ready to explain the reason for the hope that lies within you." — Saint Paul

In *GET GLOWING! You Are a Star Right Where You Are*, I heed Saint Paul's admonishment and explain the reason(s) it has been possible for me to endure thirty years of the physical demands of life on the road; the mental challenges of working in the corporate world, including an acquisition, earthquake, and a move from California to New York; the emotional pains of love lost and gains of worldwide friendships; the financial rewards of practicing the lesson "It is more blessed to give than receive"; and the peacefulness of serving in strategic diplomacy in the world of the salon professional.

In the course of my explanation, you'll discover how

profoundly my devotion to God and my Christian beliefs feature in those reasons. Just know that I understand that whereas I find inspiration in the Bible, you might find it in the Torah or the Qu'ran; whereas I find solace in the scriptures, you might be comforted by the great philosophers; whereas I find joy in my faith, you might find it in nature. I trust that you, in turn, can take what I offer from my perspective, filter it through your own convictions, and reach those same truths that are personal to me yet universal in their application.

For me, it all starts with the promise that "With God All Things Are Possible," which, printed and framed, hangs on my wall in my 502-square-foot New York apartment. This oasis, affectionately dubbed "The Pod" by my dad, has become a refuge from the noise of the city and of my life on the road.

The plaque and its message, written in proper old English script, have been a part of me since I can remember. First adorning the home of my mother's parents, the Bearingers, in Michigan, it was transferred to the homes where I grew up, and now to my adult home. Its promise has been demonstrated through the lives of my grandparents and parents, and now—hopefully, thankfully—through me.

I believe it. However, there was one major life event that not even God could make possible because of my stubbornness. It happened nearly three decades ago when I could have accepted an offer to get a book published, but I let my pride get in the way. The man who could have made it happen was Johnny Bench, the Hall of Fame baseball catcher. In the late 1970s, Johnny had just published his autobiography, *Catch You Later*, and we'd become acquainted through a series of serendipitous events.

Pride And Procrastination

My father had four daughters and always said, "I got my girls at the hospital, and I'll get my boys at the altar." Growing up with him and his intense interest in playing and watching sports made my sisters and me avid sports fans, too.

To be sitting with Daddy on Saturday nights, chomping on popcorn and watching the fights (sponsored by Gillette, "To look sharp and to feel sharp too . . ."), was the best hour of the week for me. As a young, enthusiastic pastor, the needs of church members took much of dad's time and attention, so to be with him in any area where sports were played was my time with him.

Being raised in small towns near Cincinnati—where baseball meant the infamous Reds—in turn meant that we were inveterate fans. I grew up in the era of Gus Bell, Joe Nuxhall, and Roy McMillan, and was thrilled when the Big Red Machine of the 1970s with Johnny Bench, Pete Rose, and Joe Morgan made their historic mark on major league baseball.

I don't know why it suddenly came to me in 1974 that I wanted to meet Johnny Bench. Perhaps because he played baseball and was single, successful, and handsome? I can remember saying a prayer that went "Lord, you created Johnny Bench and you created me, so I know it's no big deal for you to get us together. I'm asking and believing it will happen." And I let it go.

At the time I was working as a receptionist at Designers' Loft Salon in Dayton, and it was just a matter of days before one of our clients, Sue Lilly, arrived for her appointment. Sue looked at me from across the reception room and squealed, "You're perfect!"

I thanked her and then asked, "Perfect for what?"

"We're having a benefit downtown this week for a little boy who has leukemia and we've invited Johnny Bench to come and emcee the event. Several of us will go out for breakfast afterward and I wondered if you'd like to go."

Would I like to go? Unbeknownst to Sue, this was the answer to my prayer. Of course I wanted to go. I suspect this was the first real awakening I had to the truth "With God All Things Are Possible."

I went to the event; I met Johnny. Following that initial introduction, there were other meetings when the Reds were playing the Dodgers in Los Angeles, playing the Padres in San Diego, and back home in Cincinnati. These meetings produced many wonderful conversations, which brings me back to the original story.

Johnny caught my vision of positive living. He called one beautiful day while I was living in Thousand Oaks, California. It was the hometown of Sparky Anderson, the manager of the Reds, and a great place for them to meet and play golf. Johnny presented the idea that we write a book. Tapping into his contacts in New York, he suggested that we secure a ghostwriter to help us. Then we'd perhaps go on a speaking tour to promote the truths housed in the pages and recount the experiences of our lives: he a kid from Binger, Oklahoma, and me a preacher's kid from Dayton, Ohio.

My life's one great regret is that I didn't accept his offer then and there. No! I had to butt in and suggest that I try my hand at writing it. Being the true gentleman that he is, he agreed and stepped back.

That was twenty-seven years ago.

That book manuscript has been held prisoner in various

incarnations in my head, in a dozen different file folders, and in computer files. Occasionally I'd release it on parole in mini-forms through handouts in global training sessions for salon professionals, in magazine articles, and in interviews.

Following motivational seminars I attended—like the fire walk with Tony Robbins, the "See You at the Top" meeting with Zig Ziglar, or a writing/yoga conference at Kripalu Retreat Center in the beautiful Berkshires—I'd be determined to finish it for sure this time. But for whatever reason, I was immobilized.

There it sat in its cell, alone and unfinished. I'd beat myself up if I chose to do something else other than sit at my computer adding to and refining the book. I'd go home at the end of the day and channel surf until all hours to lose myself in television programs; or I'd spend an entire Saturday at the gym or a yoga class. I'd become so engaged in my work or my family that I was just too busy to give any quality time and energy to its completion.

Sound familiar? Has procrastination ever held you hostage to that which you really know needs to be done, and yet it seems to always get put on the backburner?

I can only imagine what might have happened if I had taken up Johnny's offer and written a book and toured with it all that time ago. But I've learned one thing these past twenty-seven years, whatever is—*is!* And whatever decision I made then was the best thing that could've happened. I remind myself of my favorite mantra: "Everything's perfect, and I'm grateful." And so I come to you now saying, "All right, all ready, it's time to get it done!"

Here's why.

Love Casts Out Fear

On the perfect fall morning of September 11, 2001, at around 8:30 A.M., I was finishing my daily devotional reading and prayers in my apartment in New York City when the phone rang. At the time I was maintaining a long-distance relationship with a wonderful man, and it was our ritual to greet the morning with each other. Before hanging up he reminded me, as always, "Stay out of harm's way and stay safe on the streets of New York." I promised I would.

At 8:45 A.M. I began gathering my things and headed out to my office at Forty-seventh Street and Fifth Avenue. Hearing a plane overhead, I thought, "They must be coming in low to LaGuardia today. Never mind." I said my morning greetings to my building's doorman, Frantz, and maintenance man, Jimmy.

Strolling up to Fifth Avenue was a joy. The day was simply beautiful. I stopped at the corner at Third Avenue and turned into the sun rising over the East River to absorb its brilliant light filling my body, mind, and soul. In my head, I sang a little Sunday school song:

"A sunbeam, a sunbeam
Jesus wants me for a sunbeam;
A sunbeam, a sunbeam
I'll be a sunbeam for Him."

By the time I got to my office at the corner of Forty-seventh I noticed the whole population of busy New Yorkers on Fifth Avenue looking southward. The taxis, normally zigzagging and honking their way through the traffic, were peculiarly calm; foot traffic was stopped on the sidewalks. Everyone's eyes were focused on the World Trade Center Towers, which were in full view.

I saw World Trade One smoking, spewing flames, and immediately flashed on the great memories this place held for me. I recalled the times that family, friends, or colleagues would "ooh and aah" at the breathtaking view of Manhattan from the famous Windows on the World restaurant. We'd all enjoy each other's company basking in the five-star service, gourmet food, and entertaining music.

I remembered many special dining experiences on the 107th floor with my REDKEN colleagues who traveled from all over the country, the world. I also reflected on the weekend of my twenty-fifth REDKEN anniversary celebration, when my parents and I had brunch and enjoyed the gospel musicians who serenaded us. So many memories of that beautiful place. Now I was watching as smoke continued to encircle those Windows.

Back on the Avenue, my colleague, Maria Cerminara, jumped from a taxi at that moment and startled me with the words, "On the radio, the news reported a plane has just hit the World Trade Center." I stood there with Maria. Soon another colleague, Cedric Fort, approached us. Looking at the shock in our faces, he said, "What's wrong?" I took his shoulders and turned him around to face the blaze.

At that moment, while we stood together arm in arm, a ball of fire burst through the second tower. What could cause this? I asked myself? Was it a bomb? No, bombs don't make that kind of fire, do they?

There was a collective gasp from all standing with us: men in yarmulkes, women with shopping bags, businesspeople with computer cases. A young woman behind us on a cell phone yelled out, "I'm a newlywed and my husband is down there. He just called to say he's okay." She burst into grateful tears. I took her, a perfect stranger, into my arms. Later I asked myself, when would I ever before have hugged an unknown New Yorker on the street? Never! But this moment wasn't like any moment I'd ever lived through. Every moment since has been unlike any other. We were all profoundly changed.

Before I could make my way into the office building, I pulled my cell phone out of my bag and dialed home. I couldn't wait to get to my desk phone; I had to call immediately, needing to make contact with my mother and daddy to let them know what I'd just experienced. "Mother, turn on CNN," I cried. "Something terrible has happened at the World Trade Center."

"Honey," she sweetly said, "I've just been reading this morning in Jeremiah where he said, 'No matter what's going on, God is in charge.'" As always, her calm resolve soothed my troubled mind. This became my prayer for the day. No matter what drama is going on around me, God is in charge. I'd repeat this to myself over and over.

As the events unfolded, surrealism turned to reality and reality into fear. Along with most of the REDKEN employees, I was dismissed to go home early in the afternoon and immediately became glued to my television. I was up until 3:00 A.M. that first night, all day on Thursday, and well into early Friday morning watching every news report and image that CNN could prepare for instantaneous broadcast. I grew to appreciate the sincerity of the anchors and the fearlessness of the reporters. I especially found solace in Aaron Brown in New York. The way he paused to reflect for a moment on the completion of a story moved me—he was feeling our pain and disbelief and sharing in the moment.

My own fear increased. Though I answered countless phone calls and e-mails with the promise, "No matter what's going on, God is in charge," and added to that, "Love casts out fear," but as a human being, an eye-witness to the events, I remained unsettled by the experience. I was a mess.

There was also the realization that I couldn't know what part of this experience God was in charge of. But there was one thing I could do: Choose to put God in charge of me! And it was from that place that I was able to go into action with those who were closest to me and do what I could to bring peace to their world.

I know that love and fear cannot dwell in the same space at the same time. So I was determined to love everyone and everything that I was faced with. Whenever my own fears arose, I realized it was because my focus had returned to *me*. I knew better. I know to go into service when the trials of life surround me like a cloud. That action always brings peace, takes the attention away from self and puts it onto someone else.

I couldn't do everything, but I could do something.

My colleague and friend, David Stanko, had been displaced from his apartment in the Wall Street area. His one desire was to have some of the peace and comfort of home: clean sheets, towels, and to take a shower in a bathroom that wasn't swathed in dust. Though my place is small, I offered my pullout couch, Chinese dinner up on my roof garden, and a long, hot, cleansing shower with fresh, fluffy towels. He accepted my invitation. And I felt that I was contributing to ending the chaos by giving one New Yorker a peaceful experience.

Another colleague, Sam Mattingly, was displaced without

her closet full of beautiful clothes. I was moved to go to the Ann Taylor store in the street level of our lobby and pick up a few choice things that she could feel fresh in. Not abundance, but thoughtfulness, was the order of the day.

A great moment of gratitude was the evening of the eleventh, when I was convinced to get ample provisions into my home. We didn't know at the time what other attacks might still be coming, so having our homes stocked with necessities was a good idea. I went to my local grocery to get the things that I thought would be both nutritional and comforting. I was loaded down with six fully stocked bags when I stopped for the light on Second Avenue.

Down the Avenue they came, like a military convoy, the skilled workers of Con Edison, my power company. There I stood, counting twenty-five trucks loaded with cables as big around as my arm, cranes, and spools of wiring. I thought, how wonderful that even in the midst of conflict there was a plan in place for disaster. There were people available and trained, supplies ready to be dispatched, and everyone knowing their responsibility when they arrived on the scene. At that moment I was grateful to be a customer of Con Edison. Every month since then, I've been happy to write the check in payment for the use of the power in my home.

By Saturday, my loving family decided I needed to get out of New York City and have a few days of R and R in Ohio. My sister Tot and her husband, Sam, were my rescue workers and drove twelve straight hours from their home near Cincinnati to pick me up. I was so thrilled to see them pull up in their van in front of my apartment building. We hugged and cried together.

I wanted to share with them a bit of our experience, so we walked the two blocks to my local fire station where we stood in homage to the ten guys who were not going to return to the house. Candles, flags, flowers, and cards took their solemn space out on the sidewalk, and passersby stopped as we did for a moment of tribute and prayer. After dinner, we packed the van and began the return trip to Ohio, delivering me to the safe harbor of my parents. Home!

My friend Johnny drove from Oklahoma and was sitting on my family's front porch waiting when we arrived at 8:00 P.M. on Sunday evening. The neighbors came out to greet us, and kids came running and waving American flags. I felt like a returning war hero. For the next week, I allowed myself to receive the tender loving care of my family and friends.

The outpouring of faith, which was broadcast worldwide, was something I never thought I'd live to see. The unified members of Congress singing "God Bless America" on the steps of the Capitol; Billy Graham at the National Cathedral; the Prayer for America service from Yankee Stadium. I sobbed when Bette Midler sang "Wind beneath My Wings." We were reminded by one of the ministers, "We will get through this." I wept when CBS News anchor, Dan Rather, broke down during his appearance on David Letterman's show while reciting the verse of "America the Beautiful":

"Oh beautiful for patriot's dream that sees beyond the years
    Our alabaster cities gleam, undimmed by human tears."

My tears flowed as Julia Roberts urged all of us to "Love one another; God is great." The words of strength and power from our president: "This is a battle between good and evil, and make no mistake about it, good will overcome"; the words of support and comfort from our governor, referring to those who lost their lives: "They would be proud"; the words of resolve and hope from our mayor, Rudy Giuliani: "We will rebuild and we will be stronger": All these words were life-giving to me during those days.

When the mayor bravely looked into the camera on *Saturday Night Live* and spoke the words, "Our hearts are broken . . . but they're beating," I felt a powerful force shoot through my body and knew it was time to resume my life. I made plans to return to my New York on American Airlines, and to walk back to my office on Fifth Avenue.

On the evening of my first day back, walking from the office to Sports Club LA in Rockefeller Center, I gasped when I turned down the block that led to the promenade.

The poles that normally flew flags of all the countries, or of some special promotion at the Center, were all so proudly waving American flags. I'd never seen that many in one place at one time. The scene literally took my breath away. Under my breath I sighed, "I love my flag."

Leaving the club and walking across Fifth Avenue at Fiftieth Street, I noticed that the windows of Saks Fifth Avenue looked strangely demure. After all, we were in the middle of Fashion Week. Thinking they had pulled the blinds and were changing the fashionable themes, I looked twice. Then I realized that every window was painted black with a message printed in white lettering that spoke for all of us—"With sadness." In the corners of the windows were beautiful sprays of white flowers of every description in gigantic vases and bathed in white light.

As my eyes turned from the windows, I got my first real look down Fifth Avenue. Instead of seeing the lighted windows in the Twin Towers holding the fort at the base of our island, there was emptiness. I was immobilized. "Where are the Towers?" I lamented. Again my tears flowed.

The next morning, another beautiful fall day, I approached the office, and looking down the Avenue I was empowered by what I saw. Never again the familiar sight of the World Trade Center Towers, but what I saw was sky! Tiffany-box-blue sky. I immediately began singing that old Irving Berlin song, "Blue Skies."

From that moment, I had a new inspiration born of the tragedy. Before 9/11 I would stand at the corner of Forty-seventh and Fifth, and proclaim that our 575 building is "The Center of Fifth," just as the bronze plaque on it declares. To my left I could see the towers of the World Trade Center, representing the treasures of the world being traded every day in the free enterprise system that we so often take for granted. Those who took them down believed the way to destroy an ideology was through the destruction of its temples. To them, the Towers represented the temple of Western capitalism, which they opposed so violently. To me, those towers were icons representing REDKEN's theme of "earn a better living."

To my right I could see Saks Fifth Avenue, St. Patrick's Cathedral, Central Park, and the Metropolitan Museum of Art—icons of the temples of the soul, representing REDKEN's other theme of "live a better life." Those responsible for the destruction of the material temples didn't count on the fact they could not destroy the American soul.

At the center of Fifth, we were helping salon professionals

learn better, so they could earn better, so they could live better. And with the Towers gone, I could no longer point to them as the icon.

When I saw the blue sky, it then became clear to me that sometimes the goals and dreams I have for my life were like the Towers. Set in my ways, set in my determination, set in my focus, I only saw the Towers ahead of me. Once they were gone I was forced to look up, to see blue sky. This meant that now my life was about not knowing what's next, not having a clear vision of where I'm headed or what's on the agenda. Simply trusting, looking upward, and living each day in the Divine "I don't know." My addiction to always having the answers was broken.

All of these experiences, and many more, moved me to finish *GET GLOWING! You Are A Star Right Where You Are*. It was just another morning when those citizens of our city were going about their lives, doing what they do, loving those they loved, earning a living, and living their lives. The one burning question that I ask myself now is, what would they say to me right now if they could? What would they advise me about any indecision or problem, anxiety, or worry that I have? Then I sit and wait for the answer . . . and 100 percent of the time, I hear those still small voices saying, "Do it now!" "Don't worry—be happy now!" "Love now!" "Get that book finished now!"

It is out of honor to those who died to reaffirm our country's faith and freedom that I'm getting this manuscript out of my head, out of the file cabinets, and out of the computer. For the firefighters from my neighborhood station, Engine 8 Ladder 2 on Fifty-first Street between Third Avenue and Lexington, I'm writing. For my building's security guard, George, whose uncle was not found, I'm writing. As George said, "He must be there 'cause he's not here." And I'm writing for my friends and colleagues Brent, Diego, David, and Mark who are fully alive yet were displaced from their apartments that at one time had a magnificent view of the World Trade Center.

And as I write with clarity of purpose, I'm singing the song my mother recited to me to accompany my Jeremiah promise:

> "Oh joy that seekest me through pain
> I cannot close my heart to Thee;
> I chase the rainbow through the rain
> And feel the promise is not vain,
> That morn shall tearless be."

I invite you to join me as we look up into the night skies, to think of those who have gone before us as the brilliant stars.

Can we be bold and courageous enough to proclaim our own glow here on earth? Will you join me in doing whatever it takes to "shine out like the stars holding out the word of life" to all who come into your world?

This is my intention for this work. I believe with all my heart . . . *You are a star right where you are!*

rise and shine!

"You are the light of the world."—Jesus

Can you imagine allowing yourself to shine without feeling self-conscious or self-centered? How would your thoughts, words, and actions change if you genuinely allowed yourself to say with acceptance, "I am a star"? Would you be willing to do the things that will make you shine? How differently would you serve others? Would you be willing to step into someone else's heart with love and leave them feeling loved and wiser?

When I began to open my heart and embrace this Divine declaration, I understood it to mean that I should have wholehearted, loving kindness for myself: Just as I am! And through the words, stories, and practices of this book, I'm encouraging you to start where *you* are and claim *your* stardom.

In the 1970s, photos from the *Pioneer 10* spacecraft were beamed back to earth. They revealed the first images of the planet Jupiter, which in mythology and the interpretations of astrologers influences spirituality, intuition, and the highest version of ourselves.

Rich in design, color, and formations, one photo was reproduced on the cover of a newsmagazine. I looked at it with a question in mind: Where had I seen this before?

I sifted through the hair research files at REDKEN Laboratories, then located in Van Nuys, California, and found my answer. It was a photomicrograph of a plug of skin taken from the hand of one of our research chemists. Under the powerful magnification of the scanning electron microscope, the image of the skin, to my eye, was identical to the image of Jupiter! My heart raced as I found science, in that moment, to be a part of the new home for my spiritual journey. I was discovering the personal truth in the quote from famed astronomer Dr. Carl Sagan, "We are made of star stuff." I also discovered, through the lens of the scope, that we even look like star stuff.

Furthermore, famed nutritionist Adele Davis noted in her book, "When you stand and extend your arms and legs, you form a five-pointed star." Think of it: The atoms of the universe move out of the way so that you can live, thrive, and shine in your unique space.

No other person can be in your space as long as you are there. No other has the right to deliberately dim the sparkle of your gifts, talents, and personality by putting you down or making fun of you. No other gets to make you feel insignificant or unworthy.

It's no longer necessary or acceptable to live your life vicariously through the lives of others, whoever they may be. Celebrities in the worlds of movies, television, music, theater, sports, or any other arenas are no more a star than you are. When you accept your own stardom and find your optimum place where your light can shine, you will then live "vicariously" through yourself. I love this thought.

As you GET GLOWING, you will contribute fully, feel fulfilled, and earn the most so in turn you can give the most. From this honest and humble place, you have the privilege of taking in the nourishment that you need in order to allow others, encourage others, and serve others to shine as the star they are, too. The message of GET GLOWING is simple: *You are a star right where you are!*

What makes it possible for any of us to shine at full wattage, and to turn "becoming" into "being," is giving daily attention to and balancing each of Five GLOWpoints.

1. Taking care of your inner and outer **body**
2. Shepherding and releasing the **thoughts** that enter your mind
3. Caring for your **relationships** with divine kindness
4. Having the right intentions in how to earn, invest, give, and spend your **resources**
5. Living in alignment with your value system; being forgiving and grateful for the unlimited love that energizes you to **serve others**

Doing something each day to achieve this balance allows you to get yourself out of the way—or, as my friend Anita Schertzer says, "put yourself to bed"—and truly be able to give attention to others. Nothing is more important than getting in touch with the core of your being—your inner "is-ness"—because then you can be in touch with the core of others. I want every person I'm connecting with in this book to leave our interaction feeling loved and wiser. And so my prayer for this work is that I will connect with you through these words and you truly will come to believe that *you are a star right where you are!*

It is not the purpose of this book, or its message, to suggest that we declare and live our "stardom" for its own sake. It's my opinion that shining as the star that you are is the first step in serving. To serve is to be number one. The last is first. To accept that you're worthy to serve, and willing to serve without reserve, begins by accepting your significance, and that begins with experiencing the truth that bears saying again: *You are a star right where you are!*

To speak or live your truth, first come the acceptance and affirmation of it. If you've had difficulty making yourself a priority, please stop here and be aware of how you feel when you say to yourself silently, "I am a star."

Now repeat this truth out loud, inserting your name below:

"I _____ am a star!"

I believe with all my heart that you can accept your stardom by making your way through the Five GLOWpoints with me. And I hope that my personal anecdotes will further inspire you, and that my poems offer some lines to live by. So, let's GET GLOWING!

1
get real

"Do everything without complaining or arguing, so that you may become blameless and pure, children of God without fault in a crooked and depraved generation, in which you shine like the stars in the universe as you hold out the word of life." — Philippians 2:14–16

The day this message broke through my clouds of fear was in the Hyatt Hotel in Kansas City; earlier, in the spring of the same year, the hotel had suffered a major structural collapse on prom night. Many young people and their chaperones were killed. In this same hotel, my spirits collapsed under a rumor I heard had begun spreading about me. One of my managers broke the news to me.

I stumbled in disbelief to my room, stretched out on the

bed, and began thinking of all the ways I could defend myself. I felt defeated. Then, just as the Fairy Godmother appeared to Cinderella in her disappointment at being rejected by those closest to her, words began flooding my mind. They formed themselves into the following poem as they urged themselves out of my fingers.

Look

Look all around you and see who you are
Look all around you you're a shining star
Where did it come from
Where will it go
Nobody's caring like you do
Nobody knows like you know

Look all around you you're walking on air
Look all around you now's the time to share
A new way of meaning
A new way to grow
Nobody's caring like you do
Nobody knows like you know

All you can see you can claim just by saying
"It's mine"
All you must do is be willing each day just to shine
Star shine

Look all around you the time is at hand
Look all around you now's the time to stand for
All you believe in
Some seeds will grow
Nobody's caring like you do
Nobody knows like you know

Taking each word and each line separately, I saw the end to my despair and defeat. I felt the end of years of imprisonment in which I'd been held captive to the lie of comparisons, captive to the ignorance of individual significance for myself and for others. As I completed the last word of the last line, I knew without a doubt that the rumor and my fear of it would pass. The truth was the promise held in the lines of the poem.

I invite you, too, to use the words of this poem as an exercise in "looking."

- **Look all around you and see who you are.** Identify, capture, witness, and glean who you are. Do a 360-degree turn. What do you see? Identify who you are by what you observe. Now there's the truth.

- **Look all around you you're a shining star.** No matter what you see, the Truth is: You're a light in that place. If you see good, you can see better. If you see negative, you can see positive. Cast light on anything that can give you a new perspective and illuminate lessons still to be learned.

- **Where did it come from?** Where did this desire to be a light, a messenger, and a servant come from? God, of course. It also came from your personal grounding, culture, and devotion.

- **Where will it go?** What's the plan for this light to shine? Where, when, on whom, and why?

- **Nobody's caring like you do.** You are unique. Ten million sperm and you won! No one else can care and have compassion stemming from your own experiences, beliefs, and values. No one can express them the way you do, so if you don't express them, it won't get done.

- **Nobody knows like you know.** This is not to say that you or I have all the answers for everybody and every situation. The Truth, however, remains. Because of your life path, nobody else can know or hold an opinion in exactly the same way. So you are entitled to your perspective and are welcome to voice your opinion without fear of loss or abandonment. I value your opinion but may not share your viewpoint. *Vive la différence!* As a matter of fact, if you don't contribute your unique perspective, you're ripping off the people around you.

- **All you can see you can claim by just saying "It's mine."** Good or bad, happy or sad, successful or disappointed, all that you see you can claim as yours. When you desire that the picture be different, then a change in you changes the view you see. Consider the Serenity Prayer: It implores God to "grant serenity to accept the things I cannot change, courage to change the things I can, and the wisdom to know the difference." Until recently, I decided that the things I could not change were externals—immutable laws, others' behavior, for instance. Then it dawned on me that what I cannot change might be totally within or about me: my predispositions, personality traits, and physical attributes. When I totally accept—with serenity—those things that I waste valuable energy and time on (like the lie of comparisons), I can truly receive the courage to change the things about me that I am able to change. I can live happily ever after in the acceptance of my total self and the experiences that are created from my living fully in my authenticity.

- **All you must do is be willing each day just to shine.** The key here is willingness. Begin each day with a heart willing to accept the star that you are, to accept others as the stars that they are, and to accept with contentment the events that take place as part of the path you're on. And shine anyway.

- **Look all around you the time is at hand.** Look around again and this time really see what's happening in the broader sense. War, rumors of war, and violence posing as entertainment are the opposites of a peaceful, positive life.. The time is at hand; the day is now. This present moment, breath by breath, we can make a choice.

- **Take some time to stand for all you believe in.** Take time to stand could simply be a pause before responding, a long slow breath to clear your mind and spirit in a tense situation, a silent prayer or repetition of an affirmation before reacting. Taking time to stand gives you a moment of personal grounding. It reminds me of mountain pose in yoga class, the fundamental grounding posture that literally grounds feet and center to the gravity of the earth. It is from this posture that real expression can occur because there's nothing that can push you off balance physically or internally. A solidly grounded feeling occurs when I take time to stand mentally, emotionally, spiritually, and physically in the moment.

Recently, a daily ritual to take some time has become a source of strength for my day. I clocked my movements from rolling out of bed in the morning to showering, prepping hair and face, and getting dressed, and discovered it's forty-five minutes. My spirit began stirring as I read Julia Cameron's *The Artist's Way* in which she recommends taking time to write three pages every morning of anything that comes to mind. It occurred to me that if I take forty-five minutes a day to prepare physically and spend zero minutes prepping spiritually, then when I leave my home and step out onto the streets of New York, it's as though my soul is naked and vulnerable. Now, the process of daily devotionals is not something foreign to me. I grew up in the parsonage, and as a daily ritual my mother would turn on a fifteen-minute radio program, *Sweet Hour of Prayer.* That program chimed with beautiful music and brief sermonettes five days a week. She then would kneel with my sisters and me and say a prayer of protection for our school day. So the idea of a daily spiritual practice was in my genes. I just had to get to a place where I could visualize this "naked soul" running around the crazy busyness of the streets of New York. I dedicated myself to the following "taking some time."

- The moment my morning chimes go off, I roll over, pick up my phone, and dial my friend Duke Duvall's "Moment of Inspiration" (800-939-5689 or www.liftinglives.com). His vibrant enthusiasm for life and his relatable knowledge of the scriptures set my spiritual course for the day.

- When I finally place my feet on the floor, I wipe the drowsiness from my eyes, find my glasses, and sit comfortably on my sofa, where I'll listen to songs from favorite CDs like Josh Groban's "Closer," Michael Crawford's "On Eagles Wings," or Barbra Streisand's "Higher Ground."
- Then I read the devotional of the day from Hazelden Press, *Daily Word*, or *Come Ye Apart*. I'll conclude with my own silent prayer, suggested by Dr. Arthur Caliandro, my pastor at Marble Church in New York: "Help me, help me, help me; and thank you, thank you, thank you."
- Finally I begin writing my three morning pages as per Julia Cameron. These jottings may include baggage from the day before, to-do lists, my mind/spirit utterances, and thoughts from mind to page.

My goal is to balance the same amount of spiritual prep time with physical prep time: forty-five minutes each. I'm not quite there yet. It's about forty-five/twenty. But since it began a couple of years ago at forty-five/five, I feel wonderful in the work that's in progress. As one of the devotionals reminds me, success is taking one positive action, nothing more. And in this daily commitment I feel successful.

One morning I was running late and made a mental promise that I'd do my devotionals when I returned home that evening. I was struck by a powerful thought that came through loud and clear; it was God speaking, "If you take time for Me, I'll make time for you." With that promise, I sat down and began my practice deliberately and mindfully. When I looked at the clock at the completion of the rituals, to my shock the hands had barely moved! God was able to stretch time so He could prepare me for the day. Design your own meaningful ritual to take some time for your spirit.

- **Take some time to stand for what you can do.** Simply taking time, sifting through expectations, letting go of "should" and "ought" and "must," and simply surrendering to the one thing you can do with all your passion is a huge relief. Rather than trying to do it all, do it with all that you have and are! I remember when Paula Kent Meehan, the founder of REDKEN, shared with me the realization "We can do anything, but we can't do everything." That was a major lesson for me. My compelling thought for you is to put your life and projects on an organizational chart and see how thinly spread you've become. Then begin to clear out, clean up, and let go of those activities that you're involved in because you couldn't say "no," or those you thought were a good idea at the time and now have become draining. It simply doesn't represent who you are now.

- **Nobody's caring like you do, Nobody knows like you know.** Can you even imagine how free you'll be when you've truly come home to the one great thing that you're designed and destined to do? The caring you've been able to demonstrate to date will take on new dimensions and outreaches. And you'll know what to do, how to do it, and when to do that special thing. You'll truly shine as the star that you are. You'll find yourself allowing others their place to shine, too!

A Path To Truth

While visiting Unity Village in Kansas City, Missouri, I walked the labyrinth. It's an archetypal symbol of wholeness that invited me into a transformative prayer experience. Walking this mystical path is a personal pilgrimage to spiritual wholeness. As I walked, I quoted silently the scripture from Jeremiah 1:4, and the sentence jumped out, "Behold I've put my words in thy mouth." I began to question God. "What new words have you put into my mouth that I haven't spoken yet?" Winding my way through the labyrinth in the peaceful rhythm of my walk, I eventually found myself at the center rosette, with six petals in which to stand. They immediately reminded me of the Five GLOWpoints, plus one.

I stood in the middle of the first rosette. "My body," I thought. "What new word do I need to hear about my body?" The word "bright" came to me. A bright body is an energetic body; it affects the people in a room when it enters. The face is bright, the eyes are bright, and the smile is bright. And then I asked the crucial question, "What do I need to do to have this bright body?" The answer was immediate and clear: "Rest." I recalled the words of my friend Barb Harris, vice president and editorial director of *Shape* and *Natural Health* magazines, "Protect and defend your sleep." I knew this was one that I had no choice but to adhere to from that moment on.

Second rosette: my thoughts. "What new words did I need to hear regarding my thoughts?" The words came to me immediately: "Clean," followed by "clear." As I meditated on these two words, the explanation was evident: "Leave behind all judgments." My thoughts can be clean and clear when I'm aware of the millions of times a day that I'm in judgment about someone or something. When I am consciously aware of living in nonjudgment, my thoughts will be only of uplifting good. Is this possible?

I moved to the third rosette: my relationships. "What do I need to be, do, or have differently in my relationships?" The word came: "Pure." Let's see if I have this right. I'm supposed to have "pure" relationships. "Show me how to do this," I implored. Then came the follow-up thought, "Simply accept everyone as they are." Period. This made sense: Since my thoughts are now going to be nonjudgmental, it would be easy to accept everyone around me—my family, my business associates, my friends, and my acquaintances—wholly and completely as they are.

The fourth rosette was now waiting: my money. This time my thoughts were completely transformed from thinking of this star point as simply my money. It was now to be thought of as "my resources." As I probed, "what about my resources?" The answer came: "Mindful giving." As in the past I've given from a generous heart, I now need to mindfully give through my investments, my spending, my saving, and my gifting. I must be ever mindful of those individuals and institutions with which I share the wealth of my time, talent, and income.

Rosette five: my spirit. The new word in respect to my spirit was to think of service, with the noun becoming a verb: "Serve us." When I look into another's eyes, I must remember that is ultimately the cry of their hearts: "Serve Us!"

The sixth rosette in the labyrinth was a bonus. What occurred was the honest revelation of sexuality and admitting how important it's always been in my life. Something I never thought I'd write about in a book. However, it has always proven to be a spiritual experience for me. And so I posed the question, "What new word do I need to hear about my sexuality?" "Real" was the response —get real. "What does real stand for?" The acrostic followed.

Rightfully
Engaging
All my
Love

For now and for the future, I must rightfully engage all my love without hesitation. I must love divinely out of a pure heart.

2

GLOWpoint one—your body

"Are you tired? Worn out? Burned out on religion? Come to me. Get away with me and you'll recover your life. I'll show you how to take a real rest. Walk with me and work with me—watch how I do it. Learn the unforced rhythms of grace. I won't lay anything heavy or ill fitting on you. Keep company with me and you'll learn to live freely and lightly."—Matthew 1:28–30

When it comes to the issues of the body, so often I'm sent messages that involve taking some kind of action: doing aerobics, stretching, weight training. While all activity leads to balance and is beneficial, I put emphasis on resting, restoring, and renewing. I believe I simply need to take moments in my day to rest and listen to my body tell me what I need to do for it.

Inspiration Rides on the Breath . . .

"God created man and breathed into his nostrils the breath of life." The word for breath is derived from the word "inspire." So when I'm tired, or creatively or emotionally blocked, all I need to do for inspiration is look to my next breath. Slow deep inspiration or inhalation, slow deep exhalation. I create my own thoughts for my thoughtful breathing exercises. They can be lines from my favorite song, a poem, or positive words or phrases.

Try this exercise for yourself:

- Take a long, slow, cooling breath in through your nose, counting to four. Fill your belly. Fill your lungs. Fill your chest.
- Hold to the mental count of four: "One, two, three, four."
- Release to the count of four through your mouth in a long, low warm sigh: "Ahhhhhhh . . ."
- Repeat twice more. But now try breathing in "joy," breathing out "fear"; and breathing in "gratitude," breathing out "forgiveness."

. . . and Resides in a Moment of Relaxation

Can you picture still water? Can you picture flowing water? Can you picture still, flowing water? Our attention tends to get caught in the frantic flow of life because we're conditioned to focus on it; thus, we don't notice the stillness. But you can train your heart center to rest in the quiet place, to know that everything is complete by remembering that no matter what's going on, God is in charge. You may not be able to see how He's in charge of what's happening *around* you, but you can allow Him to be in charge of what's happening *inside* you in order to cope with the circumstances.

Finding time to enter your own personal quiet place creates "resting awareness." Stillness heals, inspires, guides, and enlightens. This is what we call the science of energy management. Your energy determines your experience. When you discover a new way of "doing" your energy, it will heighten your way of "being" your energy.

Read through the following relaxation technique. And then proceed. Even better, have a friend or loved one read through it while you participate, and then switch to give them the same chance to relax. No solution eludes a quiet, expectant mind.

- Close your eyes and instruct your eyelids to relax. Did you feel your entire body going limp? If not, tell your eyelids to relax again. Feel the release happening from your shoulders all the way down to the tips of your toes. Ask your shoulders, "Where are you?" Drop them; allow gravity to release them. In stressful times, shoulders rise unconsciously, carrying undue stress and tension.

- Take a slow, deep breath in to the count of four, and out to the count of four.

- Now repeat to yourself silently the word "content." What does the word "content" mean to you? Can you define it without any notion of guilt or laziness? The degree that you've allowed yourself to experience this relaxed feeling is the degree to which you allow yourself to feel contented. And to feel contented is to be in the present moment: A place where you can listen to a lesson from your body, because your body knows what it needs.

- Begin a journey through your body, and for the moment be grateful to every part: every cell, every tissue, every muscle, and every organ. Be grateful for your hair, eyes, mouth, and teeth. Be grateful for your brain, neck, shoulders, chest/breasts, heart, and lungs. Be grateful for your stomach and your intestines. Be grateful for your internal organs including your spleen, pancreas, adrenal glands, liver, kidneys, and bladder. Be grateful for your spine, pelvis, and reproductive organs. Be grateful for your thighs, knees, calves, ankles, feet, and toes. Whatever state they're in, be grateful. Thank them for their faithful service to you.
- Speak kindly to your body. Breathe into that area that carries pain, aches, and tightness. Bring fresh breath—inspiration—to those places.
- Repeat the following phrase as you gratefully review your body, "Everything's perfect, and I'm grateful."
- Now retrace your body mentally by asking the question, "What is God's highest version of my body?" Stay quiet. Listen as the still small voice gives you the answer. Acknowledge and devote yourself to what you "hear." You may be prompted to exercise your body more, better, or differently. You may be prompted to select different kinds of foods. It may begin to give you an appetite for those foods that will serve you better. You may be prompted to take in more water, vitamins, or fresh air. You may be prompted to get more sleep, or take rest breaks during the day. You may be prompted to

invest time and money on your eyes to improve your sight, your teeth to improve your smile, your spine to improve your posture and circulation, or your feet to improve your stability and agility. You may be prompted to play! You may be prompted to engage in "sacred pampering"—to revel in the unique flesh that houses your life energy and allow a caregiver to do just that—give it care.

• Before coming out of your relaxed state, have your companion read the following:

Peace the opposite of tense
Peace when nothing makes much sense
Peace like the sunset at the beach
Peace and to think it's in my reach

The Body Is Coagulated Thought

To change your body is to change the thoughts you have about it, and the ways you habitually speak about it: "My big thighs, my flabby arms, my wrinkled face." Change the thoughts and speech, and it will begin to change.

To change my own body, I rest, relax, and ask it questions. I speak to it differently, and I speak about it differently. If I'm directed to engage in activities at the gym, such as lifting weights to increase muscle mass and improve strength, I use positive words rather than numbers to count.

May I make a suggestion that makes counting those repetitions a more meaningful experience? Instead of silently counting "1–2–3–4–5–6–7–8" in your quest for toning and defining, choose some positive words that will strengthen your spirit's resolve such as "love, life, beauty, order, perfection, aliveness, abundance, prosperity, sensuality, sensitivity, wisdom, wit, health, rhythm, movement, flexibility, style, dignity, grace, elegance"—or anything else you want to affirm. I find myself silently repeating these words also as I climb and descend stairs, or anytime counting begins to occupy my thoughts.

The Body Knows

My longtime friend, Leopold Bissonnette from Montreal, shared a majestic moment with me regarding talking with and listening to my body. We were in a room where a large, plate glass mirror hung on the wall opposite to where we were standing. He pointed to my reflection in the mirror and said, "Have you ever taken a look at her and asked her exactly what she wants? You've traveled around the globe, helped others to define and achieve their life's dreams. Have you ever asked Ann what she really, really, really wants?"

Embarrassed to admit that I never had, I mumbled something about setting goals in a motivation class, writing them down, and carrying them with me for years. "No," I said. "I've never asked the one person who means the most to me what she really, really, really wanted in life."

Leopold smiled. "She knows. And if you sincerely ask her, she'll tell you!"

It took me nearly a month to get the nerve to stand before my own mirror because I knew Ann would answer honestly. I wanted to make sure I was ready to hear her answer. One Sunday morning, I looked intently into my eyes in the reflection in the mirror.

I began, "Annie, honey, I love you very much. I want to give you exactly what you really, really, really want in life. But I don't know what that is."

And then I shut up.

From the depths of my stomach came a feeling that began to move up, up, up until it stuck in my throat. Surprising me, it continued to the place where the burning begins behind my eyes, and tears formed and dropped onto my cheeks. Annie began to speak. "All I ever wanted was a home."

When I could, I began to speak. "You mean I've taken you around the world, toured the wonders while staying in beautiful hotels, and eaten in five-star restaurants, and all you ever wanted was a home?"

She nodded her head. "Yes."

"Okay. I'm going to do everything I know to do to give you a home."

Standing before that mirror that day revealed an answer, one of a lifestyle choice: "All I ever wanted was a home." However, you can use this method to find out what your body is willing to have and provide for you.

- Look into a mirror, focus on your eyes, and ask the questions "What can I do for you?" "Who can I get to assist me with doing this for you?" and "When do you want me to start doing this for you?"
- Your body knows what it requires and when it requires it. And it will tell you; you just need to be willing to follow its direction.
- Be faithful and watch what happens.

I check in with myself occasionally. Am I on too much overload? Have I given my body an excess? Does this feel gentle? Remember, love is a gentle thing.

NOTES ON MY GLOWING BODY

Glow Question: What image do I want to project? What will it take for me to create that image that my body really, really, really wants?

3
GLOWpoint two—your thoughts

"Do not be anxious about anything . . . finally,
whatever is true, whatever is noble, whatever is right,
whatever is pure, whatever is lovely, whatever is
admirable—if anything is excellent or praiseworthy,
think about such things."—Philippians 4:6–9

If the truth were known, my work with REDKEN began out of a dark ending to a tragic story—love entwined with business. Digging too deeply into the memories would only muddy the story and lives again, so I'll simply say that out of devastating loss, I found my work and life at REDKEN.

REDKEN began as a job and turned into my work, my calling, and my mission. I've found that there's a big difference between having a job and having "work." In my trainings across the globe, I implore salon professionals to find their "work" while doing their job. Mine was defined by close encounters of a spiritual kind, and by the guided words of REDKEN's founder Paula Kent Meehan.

It was 1972, following my divorce from my college sweetheart, and I took my daddy at his word when he said, "If the bottom ever drops out, you can always come home." Making contact with a former high school classmate, I was invited to be the receptionist in her new salon a couple of days a week until I could decide what I'd do "when I grew up."

Those two days a week became five. The weeks passed quickly, and soon I celebrated a year of working with this creative group of stylists and our faithful clients. I loved the atmosphere and social climate of the salon. It was a great experience to watch people, particularly women, routinely check in carrying the weight of the world on their shoulders and reflecting that weight in their look. Within a brief time, I'd witness them leaving with a new hair design and a fresh attitude to match.

The idea of my making a career in the salon business must have been a deep, unconscious thought. Something from my childhood, perhaps? The sights, sounds, and scents of a beauty salon weren't new to me. From the time I was three years old and my best girlfriend and neighbor, Ginny Boone (she was six), proceeded to cut my bangs, the salon has been a familiar place.

I can recall entering our house from the front porch and hearing the swinging screen door slam behind me. Mother took one look at me, grabbed me in her arms, and walked briskly to the nearest barbershop. A red, white, and blue barber pole was twirling outside as I was abruptly seated on the wooden slab placed across the barber chair armrests. I don't recall that I was crying or scared; we were just doing what needed to be done. There wasn't much to work with, but the barber did his best to get the bang disaster straightened out.

From then on, the salon was a place where my parents would invest in my three sisters and me for cuts and perms throughout our childhood. It was important that we were always presentable, and our hair was the crowning glory.

Bethel, Ohio, population 2,500, was very much like the village in Thornton Wilder's famous play *Our Town*. With a wonderful pastor (my dad) married to a popular high school English teacher (my mom), our church was on the fast track, growing with people from all walks of life and especially the high school kids, including the entire varsity basketball team.

The local hairdresser, Betty, was in Hamersville within a few miles of Bethel. She served us well, especially around the holidays. They were the highest churchgoing days of the year, and we always got new hair and new clothes to celebrate. I loved going to Betty's little salon, one room with two styling vanities, a big Coke machine, and hood dryers. I can still recall the smell of perms and hairspray, feel the knitted pink or blue roller cap she'd place over the perm rods to keep them in place, and her little drawer where she kept her day's intake of cash.

As my sisters were being served, I'd pretend that I was at the front desk taking care of the salon while Betty took care of the customers. That was when I was eight years old: a foretaste of my life to come.

Years later, when I was taking care of the front desk for real at Designers' Loft, there was one person who could see my potential to contribute. That was the man who visited our salon weekly, REDKEN's sales consultant, Bob Richman. Bob saw something in me and took a risk to recommend me for a position that he told me I "was perfect for." He made a call to our regional manager, Bill Gray, and after two positive interviews, I was hired in April 1975. I began my career as a field representative on a salary of $11,000, in a new division—the Nutralon Division—dedicated to selling nutritional products: vitamins, minerals, and protein powder especially formulated to develop healthy hair, skin, and nails from within. Great idea . . . ahead of its time.

Having graduated from Southern Nazarene University with a degree in home economics with a focus on nutrition, coupled with the training I received from REDKEN, I felt qualified to take on this job. I begin calling salons to set appointments for nutrition classes. Think about it: In 1975, Joe Weider and Jack LaLanne were probably the only two major forces in health and fitness. But here I was, living on the road, driving from one end of the country to the other encouraging hairstylists to sell the benefits of healthy hair, skin, and nails to their clients with concepts they knew little about. That's where I came in. It was my job to teach them nutrition, to tell them about amino acids and vitamins and minerals. It was a long shot, but it didn't take us long to see that unlike the hair care products we manufactured, nutritional supplements weren't going to be profitable for the salons or for REDKEN.

The decision was made to discontinue the line. After two years of living on the road out of Holiday Inns, I would be out of a job. What was I going to do? I was anxious about everything—which is contrary to the promise written in the verse printed at the beginning of this chapter.

I went to Paula. In her visionary way, she spoke to me the words that would change my life forever: "Why don't you change your message from 'you are what you eat' to 'you are what you think,' and present motivational and inspirational messages to hairdressers?"

In those days there were few women on the education teams, with the rare exception of hair colorists or the occasional haircutter/technicians. The main presentations were done by handsome, charismatic men. They were talking to predominantly female audiences, and they were very successful in selling the products and our concept of Beauty through Science.

Then here I come . . . a woman! Would the audience have attitudes about females that could block the message I would present? I recall the first presentation after my Nutralon days at our business seminar "The Challenge of Success" in Cambridge, Massachusetts. My theme took the word "beautiful" and gave it new meaning: Be you to full . . . be yourself to the fullest.

Attaching an action step to each letter of the new meaning, I made an acrostic in which I implored and directed each stylist in ways to take care of her or himself.

Begin each day with time for you.
Eat food that gives you energy.

Yes! To life.
Open up—admit your vulnerabilities.
Unforgiving is aging.

Touch in appropriate ways.
Offer what you can give, and accept the offers of others.

Face-to-face, eye-to-eye makes the connection.
Utilize all your gifts and talents.
Listen with all you've got.
Love is all you need.

I turned the focus from them always caring for the client to the unexplored waters of caring for themselves first . . . then the client. It was new. And it received some welcomed reviews.

Jobs, Careers, Callings, and "Work"

From that first program—where I met with some resistance from my own team rather than the audience—I began to find my "work": to be an unconditional encourager to salon professionals. My "work" was then confirmed by listening to the "still small voice" one night in a lonely hotel room in Portland, Oregon.

Wondering if this new career was what God really wanted for my life, I asked the question before I went to sleep. I was ready for happiness and fulfillment; not some job that would simply feed my ego and keep me on the road in strange hotel rooms, driving across the country in the dark of night, meeting strangers every day of my life. I turned out the lamp next to my bed, and snuggled into the warmth of the blankets and the soothing pillows. And then came the familiar sense of falling into that "twilight zone" as my body gave way to the mattress below me.

I heard a faint voice in the recesses of my mind. "Look," it said.

"Look?" I asked. "Where do you want me to look?" I lay there silently waiting for the next nudge. "Maybe "look" means Luke. Maybe there's someplace in Luke I'm supposed to look," I thought sleepily. Then the numbers came: four, one, seven. By following the guidance and not pooh-poohing it as just a crazy thought, I found the foundation on which I would build my life's work.

Excitedly I turned the light back on, pushed back the covers, and trotted over to the dresser drawer where I knew I would find a Bible placed by the Gideon Society. (They are so faithful, the Gideons. No matter where I've ever been in the world, in hotels, in planes, or on the sea, I found solace knowing that I would have the companionship of the Bible.)

I found my way through the New Testament, Matthew, and Mark to Luke. Then my heart started beating faster as I looked up the fourth chapter, seventeenth verse.

> *"The book of the prophet Isaiah was handed to him, and he turned to the page where it was written: The Spirit of the Lord is upon me, for he has anointed me to preach good news to the poor; He has sent me to heal the brokenhearted; To uplift the downtrodden; To preach deliverance to the captives and recovering of sight to the blind; To preach the acceptable year of the Lord. And he closed the book and gave it to the minister and said, this prophecy has come true this day. And the eyes of all of them that were in the synagogue were fastened on him. And they were amazed at the gracious words which proceeded out of his mouth."*—Luke 4:17–22

Closing the Bible, I said out loud, "Oh no! I'm being called into the ministry and I don't want to do that!"

I was resistant, thinking that the only kind of ministry was to have a church somewhere and be the shepherd of a human flock. I then heard the little voice say, "Ann, you are in the ministry. The people in the beauty industry are attracted to everything that is important to the outer appearance. When they come to the seminars sponsored by REDKEN, they'll be expecting familiar presentations on hair. You will bring the perspective of inner beauty, which is born of individual love, compassion, joy, and equilibrium."

I accepted His calling as my life's work. I had no idea at the time where this "ministry" would take me. I took to heart the message from Luke 4:17.

Just a few months later while in Washington D.C., the day before the first program I was solely responsible for was to begin, I found myself again in my hotel room asking God for direction—for the program, for my life.

I pulled the drapes and lay down on my bed with no intention to sleep, but rather to focus on what was ahead. As before, the still, small voice sounded clearly. I wouldn't say I could actually "hear" it, like someone was there talking to me; it was more like a whispering hunch. This time it directed me to Jeremiah, first chapter, fourth verse:

> "Then the word of the Lord came unto me saying,
> "Before I formed thee in the belly I knew thee; And
> before thou camest forth out of the womb I sanctified
> thee and ordained thee a prophet to the nations."
> Then said I, "Oh, Lord God, I cannot speak for
> I'm only a child."
> But the Lord said unto me, "Say not I am a
> child. For thou shall go to all that I shall send thee,
> and whatsoever I command thee thou shalt speak.

Be not afraid of their faces, for I am with thee to deliver thee," saith the Lord. Then the Lord put forth his hand and touched my mouth, and the Lord said unto me, "Behold I have put my words in thy mouth. See I have this day set thee among the nations and kingdoms to root out, and to throw down and destroy, to build and to plant."—Jeremiah 1:4–10

There was no doubt after reading this that my life, my work, and my future were wrapped up in this scripture. All I had to do was say, "Yes." And I did. And I am. And, as Bill Withers sings, I will continue "until you use me up."

Whenever I have moments of anxiety that threaten to strip my confidence, I rely on these two powerful affirmations. The third such verse I received later, around 1986, which further cemented the calling. It was back to the New Testament, where Paul the apostle confirmed this.

"Being confident of this very thing, that He which hath begun a good work in you will perform it until the day of Jesus Christ."—Philippians 1:6

Every presentation that I've made to groups on the planet from Tokyo to Toronto, from Santiago to San Diego, from Atlanta to Anchorage, from Caracas to Cape Town, and from Sydney to Seoul has begun with quiet time where I read these scriptures, affirmed their truth for me, and then surrendered, trusting that whatever needed to be said would be said.

There have been times when I was surprised at what I felt prompted to share. I believe that I've been faithful to the promptings and opened up to share the good, the bad, and the ugly. If there's anything I've learned, it's that all of us have lived with feelings of insignificance, failure, and disappointment. When I've allowed these times of my life to bubble up in my presentations, a sweet acceptance of the group would wash across the room. As Zig Ziglar always observed, "Everyone you meet is in some level of personal pain; physical, mental, emotional, financial, spiritual." So when I let the groups know I experience what they do, we automatically bond.

One story that connects every time is when I admit to making a stupid mistake. Come on, we've all had those moments when we just wanted to crawl in a hole.

One of mine happened in Puerto Rico at REDKEN's National Sales Meeting held at the Rio Mar Hotel and Casino. I mistook two chocolate gambling chips for the real thing—another of some gifts I'd already received on the trip—and tried to cash them in so as to buy a first birthday gift for my favorite boy, Jack. Yes, I wanted to crawl under the carpet. The cashier was so great when he said, "Don't feel bad. You're not the first!"

This story has served me well in helping people I meet one-on-one or in a group to see that we're all on this path and no matter how many prayers you pray, how many hymns you sing, and how much yoga stretching you do, we all do dumb things.

There have also been instances when an audience member will thank me for something I've said, and I honestly don't remember it coming out of my mouth. I think many times their own thoughts are triggered by something from me, and they'll give me the credit. What I do know is that I now have the courage to speak my truth. And it's making a difference in the quality of my life and in others' lives, proving what Tony

Robbins quoted during my experience of the fire walk in Sydney, Australia: "The quality of my life is in direct proportion to the quality of my communication."

Don't let your desire to do your "work" cause you to neglect your family. If you do, your mission may degenerate into a quest for personal importance, and your family will suffer the consequences of your neglect.

Those whom God finds faithful in small things will be trusted with greater things.

Why am I sharing all this with you? I believe everyday conversation is a presentation. And we can be in our "work" with each person who is brought to our path. The Spirit prepares them for the interaction just as we are prepared to receive them. And this is exciting. Since everything we have and will have comes through others to us, it's vital to remember to stay open, honest, and inviting so that we can give them what they need in the moment, and we can receive what we need from them in the moment. Our work is our spiritual practice. And it's time for us to recognize and allow the duality of "professional and personal life" to simply become our "life," and see how the spirit wants to live and breathe and move in each of us every moment of every day.

So you can see, from the early days of anxiety to a lifelong calling, I have been led by the powerful and truthful words of my friends, Paula Kent Meehan, Luke, Jeremiah, and Paul.

I Am What I Intend

Have you ever had thoughts of inadequacy? I have. Sometimes I still do. What I know for sure is that the attitude I choose affects my effectiveness. I will never possess what

I'm unwilling to pursue.

There's one time in particular that I learned a way to separate my "self" from my fearful thoughts and surrender to the truth of my own glow. It happened while visiting New York City—a traditionally intimidating environment in and of itself. This was more than twenty years ago, before Joan Lunden was named the new co-host of *Good Morning America* on ABC. I mustered up the confidence to call the producer of the show to inquire about auditioning for the co-anchor position.

I believe that when we have an idea, we are also given the power to take action on the idea and make it come true. I believe this because the Divine urge is God nudging me to admit that I'm ready for the highest and greatest experience of God through me.

So I dialed 411 for directory assistance, and proceeded to dial the number I was given. The ringing began on the other end of the line. Suddenly, I was attacked with a severe case of "What Ifs."

"What if . . . they think I'm stupid?"

"What if . . . they want me to leave my job at REDKEN and move to New York?"

"What if . . . they ask what broadcast experience I've had?"

With every ring of their phone, the anxieties mounted. I quickly hung up before anyone could answer. Stepping away from the phone, I began to rebuild my confidence by saying to myself, "What's wrong with me? I speak to people all the time. They can't even see me! Why am I so afraid to make this call?"

Have you ever lived this same drama? Do you know what I was feeling with my heart pattering and my hands clammy? When was it? What issue were you dealing with, and how did you resolve it?

Just prior to this trip I'd finished reading the book, *Big You Little You*. It was a guide to finding and befriending the five-year-old child who lives inside us. That child influences us more than we can imagine when it comes to asserting ourselves in unfamiliar experiences.

I pictured my five-year-old Annie. A preacher's kid, she was a performer before she was a child. Singing in Sunday school programs before the entire congregation, her first little piece went:

"I never spoke a piece before, I hope I see it through;
I wish a Merry Christmas, to you and you and you."

Public performing in the expected perfection of the parsonage family seemed to be a natural gift. Her first song in public rang with early accountability:

"I don't have to wait until I'm grown up
To be loving and true.
There are many little deeds of kindness
That each day I can do."

The performance was sound. The image was comical. Her mommy would cut her hair over the kitchen sink using sewing scissors. The easiest style was a Dutch-boy, straight-banged-bob that was shampooed with Prell on Saturday nights and neatly bobby-pinned on each side so there would be a bit of curl for Sunday morning.

At two years old, she tripped on sister's plastic dishes on

the basement steps and tumbled down, escaping injury except for the missing tooth that took forever to be replaced by her big girl tooth in front.

In addition, Annie spoke and sang with a lateral lisp. This meant that when she would say the "S" sounds, they would slip from the sides of her mouth and often spray spit over anyone near her. Her lisp was the source of embarrassment. It gave her friends a great reason to make fun of her.

Poor little Annie. A Dutch-boy hairstyle with the side curls sticking out, a missing tooth in front, and a juicy lateral lisp . . . this was the child calling *Good Morning America*.

That day in that hotel room, I was determined to work through the anxious thoughts of Annie, and I acted on the advice of *Big You Little You*. Slowly, gently, I began at my feet and visualized lifting Annie out of my body and setting her on the chair in front of me. I stepped around in front of her and knelt down. Looking softly in her big eyes, I began speaking to her.

"Annie, honey, I love you very much and I know you're afraid to call *Good Morning America*. It's okay for you to be afraid because you're little and you don't know how to talk to big people. But I do. So I want you to stay here while I go to the phone and make the call. When I'm finished I'll come back and get you, okay?"

I visualized Annie sitting there, rubbing her teary eyes and swinging her little chubby legs. "Okay," I imagined her to whimper. I went to the phone; the adult Ann picked it up and dialed the number.

This time I let it ring. This time I let them answer. This time none of the "What ifs" distracted me. This time I simply allowed the Divine Urge.

I didn't get the job. Obviously.

That really wasn't the point. I believe God simply wanted me to know that I could separate Annie's childlike anxieties from taking action on the ideas that He plants in my heart: Inspired Intention—talking to the person inside of me that's scared, and giving her confidence for interaction.

Do you remember what you looked like in kindergarten? Picture that little five-year-old and know that he or she lives within you still.

Where have you been procrastinating because of possible childlike fear? Can you picture your child sitting in front of you? Can you imagine speaking words of love and comfort to him or her? Can you see yourself proceeding to do what the adult in you longs to do?

> **Wayne's Story**
> Wayne was fired from his job and spent the next three weeks wallowing in self-pity. He didn't get out of bed. He thought he couldn't face the day. One morning the story of Annie, which he had heard me tell years before, popped into his mind. He called to tell me his story.
>
> "I remember getting out of bed and walking to our living room where we had these great, overstuffed chairs. I lifted little Wayne out of my body and sat him in front of me, just as you had told us to do. I told him I was going up to my office to make some phone calls and would be there until I scheduled three appointments for job interviews. I told him to sit there until I came back, successfully completing the task that I had been fearful of doing before.
>
> "And then, Ann," Wayne continued, "I turned the television on for him to watch while I was gone! It didn't take long. I was soon back downstairs, rejoined my adult self with little Wayne. In a short time I was working again. Happy and productive."

Remember the lyrics from "Whistle a Happy Tune," that great song from *The King and I*? The happy tune I "whistle" is the sound of myself speaking to my inner child. When I feel afraid to take action, I'm reminded that those thoughts come from my child within. She will always be with me. Now I have a method so I can see and talk to her, and calm her fears. I have the choice. Either I allow her to paralyze me with her thoughts generating from fear—thoughts of impatience, nagging worry, doubt, tension, guilt, lack, judgments, criticism, cynicism, jealousy, envy, and inadequacy—or I let my adult take action from a place of love, which generates life, beauty, order, generosity, abundance, service, grace, humor, dignity, forgiveness, honesty, and gratitude.

Love and Fear

There are only these two emotions: love and fear. The most important thought I'll ever have is the one I'm having right now. Is it coming from love or fear? Remember that love eliminates fear.

The present moment is the only moment when love is fully engaged. Fear dwells from the remembrance of past; doubt dwells from the shadowed expectation of the future, the "What-Ifs." However, if you're afraid of tomorrow you may not realize that the past is just as dangerous.

Right now, ask yourself this question: "How fully can I be in the present?" The more fully present, the more fully loving. The more fully loving, the more fully serving. The more fully serving, the more abundantly gifted with confidence to act.

It's your choice: love or fear.

Choose love.

Where I am on my journey has been flavored by the dominance of one of these two choices. That is all. The conditioning with which I was raised caused impressions on my young mind. The impressions have created a lifetime of desires. Every thought is a desire. So whatever dominates my thinking dominates my desires. My desires move me into action. And my actions cause the continuation of my impressions, reconfirming my conditioning.

It's a cycle. And if it's working for me and the "mirror" of my life is showing me what I really, really, really want to see, bravo! If it isn't, then the cycle needs to be interrupted permanently, somehow, someway.

In the high-performance team training offered to the senior management team on which I sit, the trainers have used the following description to make this same point. "A core limiting belief is a story I tell myself that sabotages my ability to get what I want."

I'm beginning to be more and more aware when I repeat a story that's keeping me stuck in a particular life stage or lifestyle. I'm also aware when I hear anyone around me telling their stories and I can quickly see how they're stuck in their own level of pain. A story very often will begin with "I can't . . ." "It's just my luck . . ." "What works for me is . . ." or any "I am . . ." statement.

I believe in asking God to delete the old, worn-out impressions and conditioning just as if He hit the delete button on my computer. I want Him to replace them with the highest version He has in mind for me. It's then my responsibility to be circumstantially aware of His guidance in everything relating to this new version. This way is the only lasting way to break the cycle and guarantee that I'll come from love for others and myself in all my desires and thoughts.

Today

Today my world is stronger
Today I can no longer
Be silent about that
Inside there's no doubt
Today
I can do more for you today

Today my future's brighter
Today the old load seems lighter
For all that I know makes me
Know that I know
Today
I can do more for you today

I am uncovering things that are hidden in me
I am discovering everything that I can be
And want to be
I feel so free

Today my world is caring
Today my world is sharing
It's great being me
Alive
Rich
And healthy
Today
I can do more for you today

It was 1978 when Clairol designed and implemented a consumer awareness media blitz that would awaken America to the benefits of professional salon stylists and services. The tag line for the campaign was "I can do more for you today."

The spokesperson for the campaign was a well-spoken industry executive who was knowledgeable and respected. I suggested to REDKEN that we create our own media tour, allow me to speak on behalf of the company, and stimulate increased business in the salons.

The tour was never blessed and thus never happened. I'm sure the disappointment and rejection of it all forced out of my fingers and onto the page this poem entitled "Today." I hope that today it can inspire you.

- **Today my world is stronger.** This present moment, let everything you know be a reflection of your stronger, more secure and confident, and more powerful-than-ever self.
- **Today I can no longer be silent about that, inside there's no doubt today.** I can do more for you today. Now, unlike other times when you've hidden behind your strengths, allow them to shine through and speak their truth. Have no doubt that you have the experience, wisdom, willingness, and discernment to choose the actions that are appropriate for your relationships.
- **Today my future's brighter, today the old load seems lighter.** The pressures, cares, tensions, and worries of the day won't seem as monumental when your perspective on yourself is bigger. The

load is lighter when you take time to surrender each day to God's will. Trust that whatever you encounter has been allowed to cross your path so that you can exercise your choices in who you want to be in solving the issue, and who you want to become as a result of that choice. My dad has always said, "God is . . . so what's the matter?" I've found that as long as you remember this, the load will be lighter.

- **For all that I know makes me know that I know today, I can do more for you today.** In this case, the first word "know" can be defined as "experienced," and in the experience comes the authenticity of knowledge. For instance, you can research a romantic tropical island, poring over colorful brochures and Internet sites that take you on a virtual tour. But there is nothing that can take the place of stepping off the airplane, feeling the balmy breezes on your face, breathing in the aromas of the flowers, and taking a bite of the native cuisine. That's when you *know* that romantic tropical island. So to know that you know, you must allow yourself to experience, so that you can speak and act and move with your own authority. In this way, others can trust your word. There is nothing more exhilarating than when you know that you know.

- **I am uncovering things that are hidden in me.** Discover the good things like talent, humor, gratitude, compassion, and tender mercies, but also those others like jealousy, fear of abandonment, rejection, or being made fun of, which block the full benefit of the good stuff.

- **I am discovering everything that I can be, and want to be, I feel so free!** What will you choose from the vast storehouse of talents: writer, singer, actress, poet, speaker, preacher, lover, friend, or encourager? You're free to choose what's right for you, what you really desire to experience, and in what measure; free to say "yes" and free to say "no"; free to be radically honest and straightforward when the issue calls for it; free to practice your life in your way; and free not to be conformed to the mob's opinion.

- **Today my world is caring, today my world is sharing.** Show love to yourself and to others; be generous with resources, time, and energy to help those who need you, for one day you may be the one on the receiving end.

- **It's great being me, alive, rich, and healthy.** Finally! Accept you, all of you, inside you, outside you. Admit to your uniqueness: No one has been like you ever before, nor ever will be again. You: Fully known and all forgiven. It's great being you! Alive, living each day fully. Rich, sensing the blessings in every person, place, and event and expressing gratitude for them. Healthy, able to dress yourself each day, put one foot in front of the other, run, play, stretch, breathe, and be alive! Alive! Alive!

- **Today I can do more for you today.** You have the

ability and willingness to extend the possibilities of relationship because in fully accepting yourself and knowing your gifts, you can fully allow you to be who you are, and allow your gifts to shine. This encourages you to do more, or all you're capable of doing without fear of being rejected or put down for being so wonderful.

NOTES ON MY GLOWING THOUGHTS

Glow Question: What has become a distraction that keeps me from growing? The extent to which my life is not working is the extent to which I'm not embracing my life. In a perfect world, everything would be as they are right now. Maybe the distractions are the gifts!

4

GLOWpoint three—your relationships

> *"Little children, let us stop saying we love people and let us really love them and show it by our actions."*—I John 3:15

The first love affair is the one where I fall in love with my*self*. I look and find what's right, and I grow in awe of the experience of life as the unique expression of God as me.

The greatest expression of this self-love is to find the right fulfillment of time for myself and those closest to me . . . letting the rest of the world fill in the blanks after that.

My friend and colleague Peter Mahoney of Halifax, Nova Scotia, has taught me much about this by telling his own story. He was type A all the way, working sixteen-hour days, smoking all day long, and thirty pounds overweight. His marriage was in jeopardy, his children living day after day without meaningful connection with their dad.

Through a series of events, Peter made a conscious choice to truly love and respect himself. He found himself staring at the calendar of the New Year that was just about to begin. He thought, what are the things in life that would bring me happiness? And he began to list them.

Spending time with my kids.
Running.
Having time with friends, laughing, and enjoying each other.
Taking ten weeks of vacation with my family.
Getting healthy.

Peter found himself plotting those activities into the calendar and making a commitment to stick to the plan as best as he could without distractions. After he was finished, he then said, "OK, world—now you can have the rest of me."

He stopped smoking and lost weight. His time with his children increased. He began running and has successfully completed more than one marathon. His running partner became his life's partner. And his businesses exceeded the annual projections.

Peter taught me to do this, too: First determining my values and visions for my life, and then making the "appointments" with myself to satisfy them and see them accomplished.

The second love affair is the one where I fall in love with others. Mother Teresa said it best: "If I spend time judging others, I have no time to love them."

Love Others as Yourself

Since I was little, I remember a Bible verse that read, "Love your neighbor as yourself." I thought it meant that my capacity to love you is equal in proportion to the love I have for myself. And that may be the way to translate the Master's words. But a greater reality came to me one day when I discovered a new way of interpreting this same command: "Love your neighbor as your *self.*"

Actually, when I look closely into the eyes of another person I can see my *self* in the dark center, the pupil, of their eyes. I may be looking at them, but I'm seeing myself.

I remember I'm not here to change who they are. I'm only here to give them what they want. What they want is to be loved, recognized, and remembered. They want to be affirmed that they are exceptional, essential, and equal. They want to belong. The very same as my *self.*

When sharing a moment with someone, I often silently say to myself, "This person matters. What they're saying matters. How they're feeling matters. There's something important at stake here." I intend to develop the conversation in such a way that they can't say "no" to my relationship to them, because I'm giving them exactly what they want: Love, recognition, remembrance, and belonging. With these, I bring them into a place of peace.

This kind of undivided, individual attention creates an interaction that can change a course of action. It's rare to have someone's complete focus in a day when it's easy to become distracted. When someone recognizes and remembers me, new life is breathed into me. I feel for those moments that I truly am alive!

To give that kind of attention is the result of physical, mental, and emotional GLOWpoints aligning. To give this kind of attention comes naturally when you've accepted that you are a star. There's no comparison with anyone anymore. No more feeling inadequate. There's nothing to prove anymore; rather, you spend your time improving these moments of life-giving attention.

One way I've experimented with improving my communication is in the area of eye contact. Although I find myself constantly wanting to make better eye contact when I'm talking, the more important contact is made while the other is talking. I developed the following theory after studying the principles of neurolinguistic programming.

We know the left brain is dominant in thoughts of a linear nature, order, logic, and verbal/numerical functions. The left brain controls the right side of the body—the right eye.

The right brain is dominant in emotional sensitivities, color, design, and vision. The right side of the brain controls the left side of the body—the left eye.

Here's my self-proven theory. When someone is speaking to me of topics emotional in nature (family, feelings, spirit, and dreams), I concentrate on looking into their left eye, since it is the path to the emotional side of the brain.

When someone is speaking to me of business, investments, or directions from point A to point B, I gaze into their right eye, since the center of logic lives there.

This makes so much sense to me. I've done it for years and have had people tell me when we're engaged in whatever topic that's important to them that they feel like I've crawled into their soul. Maybe I have. You can do this, too.

The other piece of connecting that I've found helpful is in shaking hands. Making sure I have a firm grip is one thing, but making sure the little webbed piece of flesh between the thumb and the forefinger is making contact with that part of their hand is important, too. Why? It's a pressure point to the heart. When I know my hand is touching this point, I'm touching their heart. They don't know why this handshake is different, but they sense it is.

There is only your relationship with your *self* that you see in the world around you. When you finally recognize that one magnificent truth, you recognize that relationship is everything.

I ask myself first thing in the morning, "Who needs what I've got?" "Who's got what I need?" I then trust the Spirit to lead throughout the day. I'm aware of "whisper signals" giving the answers.

Every conversation teaches me what I need to learn. Others accept me to the extent that I accept them. They open up to the degree that I open up to them. I look at that person as a mirror of my *self*. Instead of focusing on my desire to dominate the conversation, I focus on their desires by asking questions and listening for my answers.

For example, instead of asking, what this discussion is doing for me, I focus on what this discussion is doing for the other person. What is most important to me becomes what is most important to you. Instead of dominating and telling everything I know about a topic, I ask them what they know about it. There's something at stake here. These are effective ways to demonstrate that I am truly interested in developing the relationship.

Give Them What They Want

You've undoubtedly heard the Golden Rule: "Do unto others as you would have others do unto you." There have been those I've known who, in my opinion, haven't fallen in love with themselves and see others as a mirror reflection. Therefore, what they think and feel about themselves produces a less than positive "doing" unto others.

I like adopting the Platinum Rule, which is simply "Do unto others as they would have you do unto them." How do I know what they would have me do unto them? I ask them! And then I am willing to give it.

My dad always said, "There are five key words to success: Give them what they want." My own version of this is, "Serve them what they want," going back to the earlier thought that they're looking at me with "serve us" in their eyes.

Keep in mind that everyone is interested in talking about what he or she does, who they know, and where they've been. You can tell what thrills someone most: It's the first thing out of their mouths the first minute you're together. Anything they bring up can open a conversation because they never tire of talking about themselves.

Tell me what you long for, and I'll tell you who you are.

In his book, *The Five Love Languages*, Gary Chapman has identified the best ways to connect with how someone feels loved. The five choices are Quality Time, Gifts, Touch, Words of Encouragement, and Acts of Service. Breathe each of these expressions of love into yourself. Which one comes up as your priority? Express that to those closest to you. Let them know. Ask them the same question. When you know what it takes for those in your circle of concern to feel loved, and when you're willing to give that to them consistently, your bond with them grows richer, fuller, and deeper.

Listen! Your quality of life has much to do with how

well you listen and how curious you are about others. Tony Robbins, famed change agent, says, "The quality of my life is in direct proportion to the quality of my communication." We commonly assume that communication means talking. The best communication is when we're listening.

My friend Steve Shapiro has made a lifetime study of what he calls "the miracle of listening." What I've learned from him is contained in his book, Listening For Success, and is a simple, two-part secret to great conversation: Ask! Listen!

Steve has also reconfigured the word "listen" to form two other practices that will engage another person fully:

Listen—Silent—Enlist.

These three words speak volumes. First he compels us to have the intention to listen, then be silent as you listen, and finally enlist the other with your attention. For more information on Steve, his books, and his training, log onto his website at www. steveshapiro.com.

Listen specifically for personal information that sneaks into the conversation. For instance, when my friend Flora told me that she and Joe, her husband, would be celebrating their thirty-fifth wedding anniversary on November 30, I made a mental note. Later, I wrote the date in my book so I could follow up when the time came and send a card or flowers. Catching those bits of information in your "heart net" as they're casually mentioned in conversation, then following through, does wonders for relationships.

Be curious. Become your own version of a CNN investigative reporter. By probing into their comments, you can help them uncover more about why they feel the way they do, or what they truly crave. As you make a point to be curious, the conversation will lead to other topics of interest. This gives the cue to others you are involved in and actively listening to them.

Take Time for Your Friends

I love the phrase "People are more important than projects."

When someone comes into my office and I'm busy at work, I stop. Most times, they'll say, "I'm sorry to interrupt you, but . . ." Or they may ask if they're interrupting me. My answer is always "no." I won't let them feel rushed. I avoid whenever possible any distractions or interruptions while we're together, such as ringing phones or e-mails waiting to be answered. My undivided attention gives them the feeling that they are my priority. People aren't an interruption to my business; people are my business.

A good story to illustrate this happened not long after I moved to New York. I found my place of worship at Fifth Avenue Presbyterian Church, located at Fifty-fifth Street and Fifth Avenue. One beautiful summer Sunday morning, sleeping longer than I should have, I rushed to get ready for church. I threw on a little hat instead of doing my hair and took off. I rushed as fast as my legs would carry me up Lexington Avenue. I passed an obvious homeless person leaning against the outside wall of a local deli. As I passed, he said, "Nice hat lady." Thrusting a dirty paper cup he was holding toward me, he continued, "Cup of coffee, ma'am?"

Not wanting to be bothered or to break my stride, I casually said over my shoulder, "Not today, I'm late for church."

The traffic light changed, and as I was walking across

Lexington Avenue the Spirit began speaking to me in near-audible tones, "What are you doing?" The light changed again and I found the voice continuing as I stepped off the curb and continued to cross the street, "You're rushing to church to hear one more sermon on "if you've done it unto the least of these my brethren, you've done it unto me." When the voice stopped, I found myself standing in front of the man again. I had completed a square—across Lexington, across Fifty-fifth, again crossing Lexington and again Fifty-fifth, and back in front of the deli, the dirty cup, and the man.

I looked into his forlorn eyes and reached into my purse. I pulled out a couple of dollar bills and, skimming his crusty hand, I gently placed them in his offering plate, the cup. "Have a cup of coffee, and a bagel, too!"

My mom calls these moments "divine interruptions." I definitely believe this one was. In responding to this divine interruption and following through with the action I knew I needed to take, I felt like I had been to church.

Allow Grief

I can easily be tempted to give advice when my friends are going through life's dramas, rather than simply being there and giving them permission to express their true feelings. When I make statements like "You should," "Don't cry," "Don't worry," or "Don't be sad," they tend to suppress their true feelings. They may forego the pain they feel and steer away from trying to solve their problems that are causing them grief. When I allow them their grief they begin to find their own answers and discover the first step they need to take. Most of the time, all they want is to hear themselves talk about what is happening.

Giving them permission invites them to come to me with what they need because I help them discover the cause, the answer, and ultimately what makes them happy.

Grief, resentment, and suppressed feelings prematurely age us. Here's a great gift to give yourself, or you can recommend it to someone who is stuck in grief. My counselor and friend Maggie Craddock gave it to me.

Draw a bath, as hot as you can stand, and pour rock salt into the water. Immerse yourself in the bath and stay there until the water begins to cool down. The salt draws out the impurities from your skin and somehow from your spirit. Dry off and wrap yourself in a warm, soft blanket. Now, crawl into your bed, bury your face in your pillow, and allow yourself to begin *thinking of* the problem that's causing your heart to grieve. Soon you'll begin to sob. The sounds that come from pure sobbing may startle you. Let yourself hear them. And sob until there are no sobs left. In the morning, you'll feel lighter. Cleansed. Fresh. Free. Nothing happens until the tears do.

Find Something to Compliment

Sincerely complimenting something personal about another— their eyes, skin, hands, or clothing, and how well they look in what they're wearing—is a sure way to establish rapport. And that can lead to relationship. Rather than saying, "That's a great dress," you now have a choice to say, "You look great in that dress." The truth is that each time you give a compliment to another person, you're also giving to yourself. Ralph Waldo Emerson wrote it best: "What we see is always ourselves."

I would say that on most occasions when I compliment someone, they'll reject the compliment. When this happens, I literally make them pause a moment, I restate the compliment, and I suggest they say a simple "thank you." In that instant, their negative pattern of not allowing themselves to receive is interrupted.

Glowing relationships come from paying attention to others as if you were others. In essence, you are others. In loving them, you're loving your *self*.

Appreciate Them and Tell Them So

When I appreciate my family, friends, and colleagues, I tell them so. Every time I see an opportunity to thank someone for something they've done, I do it. I stop, look at them eye to eye, touch them in some way, and tell them how much I appreciate who they are and what they've done.

My friend Ron Mercer was a lifetime executive with Xerox. For part of his career, he led the Canadian Xerox team. With only a few thousand employees, the Canadians were recognized with outstanding sales awards, outproducing other major Xerox companies worldwide.

I asked Ron how they accomplished this amazing feat. He replied, "We have a great team and they have excellent product knowledge. I guess if I were to boil it down to one thing, it would be that I appreciate my people and I tell them so. That includes the secretary and the maintenance crew that cleans the offices. Everybody. As they're leaving the office for the evening, I say, 'Thanks for the day.' I believe gratitude makes all the difference."

Appreciation takes what is great in others and makes it your own.

Another way to show appreciation is by taking a small

gift when visiting someone's home. I learned this from my friends in Iran. They would never think of entering a friend's home empty-handed. Leaving something behind to remind them of our relationship extends my presence in their world long after I've gone.

What I bring is not as important as bringing it. Fresh flowers, fruit, or a card are lasting reminders. Showing appreciation and respect for others comes in ways that, over time, strengthen the trust factor, the cornerstone of relationships.

Follow Through on Commitments

We've heard it, and it's as true as ever: Under-promise . . . then over-deliver.

One of my friends in the salon industry, Jon Prill, capitalized on opportunities and became enormously successful. I asked him what he considered the secret to his success. He thought for a minute and replied, "I do what I tell them I'm going to do."

"That's it?" I questioned. It seemed so simple.

"That's all they ask for," he continued. "Most don't follow through with what they promise, so I've been ahead of the game and it's been profitable for me."

So simple.

Return Calls Promptly

Being prompt in returning messages, whether on voice mail, e-mail, or any other means, helps in developing relationships. In our lightning-speed world, where decisions and plans need to be made quickly, the "urgent" return of a call just may be what they're waiting for to clinch an important deal or to simply progress with their plans. It may not seem that monumental to you. To them, something very important could be at stake.

Sherry Lansing, chairman of Paramount Pictures, many years ago, stated on a Pacific Bell television commercial that she was committed to answering every day's phone calls by the end of the day. Those thirty seconds made such an impression on me as I thought, "If Sherry Lansing can return daily calls with her busy schedule, there's no excuse for my not at least attempting to do the same." Since then, for at least the past ten years, I've finished the day with most, if not all, phone messages—and now e-mails—returned. It feels good to know that others aren't waiting for my input or response to proceed.

Be First

My most practical lesson from motivational speaker/author Zig Ziglar came in eight short words: "If I'm not ten minutes early, I'm late."

It's a matter of respect. Showing up on time, being the first to arrive, shows I've supreme respect for colleagues, family, and friends. I set my watch ten minutes fast and am the first to arrive to greet everyone. There's power there.

I'm first to express and extend my hand and a smile when entering a room, when meeting someone for the first time, or when there is a rift between me and someone else. It reminds me of what Dr. Tom Johnson, of the Church of Religious Science, taught me: "I only have what I express. I only have what I extend." The world is my mirror.

Encourage Others

As you grow in the realization of your glowing star, you'll soon begin to realize that everyone has his or her special place to "shine." Their place, mission, and talent have nothing to do with you. No one can keep your unique gift from you, nor could or would you want to keep theirs from them. With that in mind, it's easy and exciting to listen to others' triumphs and success stories, to celebrate with them and encourage them on their way.

These actions take nothing away from your own star glowing. It bonds you to your relationships. It's so great to live free of the lie of comparisons. Because comparing is a lie. The only comparison allowed comes from Lloyd John Ogilvie, former chaplain of the U.S. Senate, when he begs to "stand at my full height and compare myself to God's greatness He intends for me to achieve."

I'm reminded of a television commercial produced in the 1960s by Equitable Life Insurance Company:

> "Is there anyone else in the whole human race
> With your kind of style and your kind of grace.
> There's nobody else exactly like you.
> There's nobody else like you."

This truth becomes the core value of my life. It allows me to join in the encouragement and celebration of others. There are times when I don't have any idea what a difference my encouragement makes. It could be a matter of life and death.

As was the case of my two friends, David and Ron.

It was a sun-drenched day in California. The kind of day when Midwesterners decide to move from their bleak, blustery towns to feel the warmth of the sun almost 365 days a year. I was returning from lunch and nearing the employee entrance to the building when I saw Ron, his carrot-red hair falling nearly halfway down his back. He worked on the sanitary production floor filling shampoos and other liquid products, so most of the time his hair was worn back and up in a hairnet. However, it was lunchtime and he had taken it down, allowing it to fly around in the warm breeze.

Passing him, I simply said, "Hi, Ron. Beautiful day!" He muttered something under his breath, making his way to his car.

The following morning when I arrived at my desk, there was a cassette tape with a note taped to it. I didn't recognize the handwriting. Opening the envelope and lifting the note out, I looked at the signature. It was signed "Ron."

Dear Ann,

Thank you for speaking to me yesterday as I was leaving the building for lunch. You'll never know what your kind smile and friendly words meant to me.

You see I was on my way back to my home to take my life. I didn't think there was anything to live for anymore and life was useless. Then I saw your face and heard your voice and I suddenly looked around. I realized "hey, you know what, it is a beautiful day." Rather than ending my life on that lunch hour, I began my life.

I've compiled a few of my favorite songs on this cassette tape that I hope you'll like. It's my way of saying thank you for your smile.

Sincerely,
Ron

Ron left his employment at REDKEN not long after that, finished his journeyman electrician training, and became involved in the construction of some of the most beautiful skyscrapers in downtown Los Angeles.

How could I know that a smile and a positive word would have that effect on that day? I couldn't. That's why it's vital that we are balanced in our own glow so that we can be available to those who are brought in our path for encouragement.

David was another story of a man on the brink. I was in Canada teaching a class on personal grounding. David made his way into the classroom to simply find some peace and quiet. I'd chosen soothing music and dim lights to greet the learners and to put them into a receptive mood for the life-enhancing topic we were going to be talking about.

He sat alone. Never spoke to another person. Shy, I guessed. What was going on inside him was the same unrest going on inside Ron. He was discouraged, disillusioned, and dysfunctional. The class began with a relaxation exercise. The group followed my instruction, taking deep breaths "in with love, out with fear." Quietly, I guided them through a relaxation technique with the objective of letting go of the stress that can so easily build up day after day in the salon.

Sometime in the course of the class, David heard me say the word "change." Just that. "Change." Simple and direct. Like the flaming arrow shot from the bow that lit the Olympic torch in Barcelona signaling the beginning of the Games, David heard the fiery word and it lit a torch within him. The next day, he sought me out to tell me what had happened.

"Sitting there relaxed and quiet, I heard the word 'change.' I've heard that word thousands of times in the past, but today— the way you said it—I was struck that I must stop complaining and being disheartened by how I am living my life. I realized no one could do it for me. And in those brief moments, I made the decision to change. Forever change and never look back. You saved my life, Ann. I was going to sit in your class and had already decided that when it adjourned I would go back to my hotel room and commit suicide. Instead, I met Holly."

That night in the Hospitality Suite, this same shy David struck up a conversation with Holly, a salon owner whom he had met a few months before. Her life was also in flux. A marriage that wasn't working, a salon struggling to be a real business. Together they talked about the status of their current lives. And they talked. And talked. Into the wee hours of the morning they shared and laughed and cried.

And they fell in love.

Within a few months, they both had made the changes they needed to make in order to be together. They announced their engagement and had a beautiful wedding in a garden. Holly and David are like two giggly teenagers in love. They combined their lives, their families, and their work. They know they were meant to reconnect with each other at the REDKEN Convention. They also know they're meant to be together, helping others find the courage and take action on the changes they so desperately need to make.

Recently, I received a card from David with a "thank you" note from one of his clients tucked inside. He had taken a few extra minutes during her salon service to give a soothing scalp, neck, and shoulder massage. The "thank you" was for more than just the tender touch. She said, "I'd broken up with my boyfriend and hadn't felt a kind touch since. Being in your chair made me feel like a woman again, and I know I'm going to be all right."

David's gift to her was to let her be who she never thought

she could be again.

The stories are endless, and the point is obvious. We are never aware of all the subtle gestures that we perform daily—without a thought—that are making an impact on those around us.

Touch with Your Heart

Touching is helpful in developing a relationship. Periodically throughout a conversation, I reach out and touch. Even for those people who are shy about physical contact, a slight touch on a "safe place" such as the upper arm, between the shoulder and elbow, is comfortable. And comforting. These touches keep a physical connection with me and send a silent message to the other person: "I'm interested and I care about you."

Study of the energy meridians of the body shows that the heart energy makes its way through the shoulders, arms, and hands. When I touch another, I'm literally touching with my heart.

And for those we feel closest to and safest around . . . Hug! Hugs can be the refreshing break someone needs that can have lasting fond memories.

It's been noted that hugging is healthy because it improves blood circulation and relieves tension. Hugging combats depression and reduces stress. It's invigorating and rejuvenating. It elevates self-esteem and generates good will. Hugging has no unpleasant side effects. It's nothing less than a miracle drug!

Some may misinterpret the gesture of a hug. To avoid embarrassment in this regard, I've started asking, "May I give you a hug?" before I assume that it's all right with them. This is known as "permission marketing," and in today's business environment asking for a hug—or anything else you want—is a smart thing to remember.

Try this for a new sensation offered by my friend Chris. When you're hugging left shoulder to left shoulder, you're hugging heart to heart. Try it. It feels awkward at first. It puts a news spin on the sometimes-routine action of hugging right to right.

What I call "self-abandoned" hugs are those when you're able to feel your body pressed fully against another's: shoulder to shoulder, chest to chest, stomach to stomach, pelvis to pelvis, thigh to thigh, toe to toe. Wonderful!

Few are willing to surrender and simply go for it. Those who do know that hugging is a great gift you give your *self* as well as someone else. And it makes you unforgettable.

I remember the first time I hugged my friend Chris. We were totally self-abandoned, feeling the fullness of our bodies all the way from our shoulders to our toes. When we released from the hug, I complimented him on his willingness to hug me so unselfishly.

Chris replied, "I have nothing to hide."

Maybe that's the secret to giving and receiving not only hugs, but everything we desire: Having nothing to hide!

Let Go

Knowing when to let go is one of the greatest lessons in relationships. Whether it's with a loved one, child, parent, or partner, the code that you've made as the star that you are may sometimes require that you let go of someone who no longer contributes to your highest good.

This point reminds me of a story of love and severe loss

because I thought this was the love that offered the promise of the home I longed for.

As a twice-divorced woman over fifty, the idea of having a home had been on my mind. Not a drastic, obsessive thought. Just there. When I received a call from a former college classmate, now living in Colorado, I thought this could be a possibility.

For three-and-a-half years, Robert and I conducted what would be considered a successful long-distance relationship in that it lasted well beyond the average long-distance lifespan of six months.

Robert's lifestyle was filled to the brim with the activities of his beautiful Colorado ranch, including the care of horses, cattle, and farm animals of all shapes and sizes. He owned property in Canada and Mexico, and was in constant motion looking after the investments, as well as his family that consisted of his three growing children, his mom, and his sisters. It was nonstop action with Robert, and I did my best to keep up. Hunting trips to South Africa, calving in the middle of the night in subzero degree weather in Canada, hiking the rough terrain of the Colorado mountainsides, and much more. From Fifth Avenue during the week to Dale Evans on the weekends, I did my best to keep up. And why? Because I thought this was the answered promise of the home that Annie said she really, really, really wanted.

Just prior to Christmas of 1999, and the highly celebrated Y2K New Year's Eve taking us into the new millennium, I came to the startling realization that Robert was committed to never remarrying. So for me to continue with the fantasy was a violation of my value system.

"If you want a monogamous, committed relationship, I'm your guy," he told me as he sat in his overstuffed leather chair in the living room at the ranch house. I loved this place. My kind of privacy away from the demands of my New York responsibilities and people, people, people. The house was nestled in the pines, the driveway three-and-a-half miles off the nearest paved road. He continued, "But if you want to be married, I'm not your guy."

Robert had actually told me, on the first weekend I visited this glorious place, that he would never be married again, after two "unfortunate marital experiences," as he called them. But, like many women, I thought he'd change his mind if I could just be enough. He'd made his declaration. I was the one who didn't hear it.

So for three years I tried to be enough. It wasn't to be. And within a few days, I boarded a flight, kissed him goodbye, and sang "Happy Trails to You." I cried all the way home.

I kept telling myself, "This is the *best* thing that could ever have happened. This is the best thing that could've *ever* happened."

Did I believe it? Did I feel it? No, of course I didn't. I held the thought anyway. Day by day. Sometimes breath by breath. I was so sad. And yet, in some strange way, I was relieved. I could breathe. And ultimately now, I can say, it was indeed the best thing that could've ever happened.

Why is letting go so difficult? It's a habit, a routine that has become part of the daily thought and action process. In order to change the familiar, new habits need to be formed. In our case, a hiatus of ninety days was declared with no communication at all.

I retreated to a solo vacation in the British Virgin Islands. Daily I'd take walks on the beach, write my cares and struggles in the sand, and stand to watch the faithful tide take them away. It was my physical way of releasing everything to God.

After reading Iyanla Vanzant's book, *In the Meantime*, I adopted a practice that I found most helpful as I followed it to the letter. It recommended that I imagine inviting Robert into my home. I was to ask him to sit down, and remain quiet. Then it was my turn to say everything I was afraid to express because I didn't want to lose him. Since I had lost him, I now felt safe to express them. Off I went, in my honesty and tears, until every point was uncovered. When I finished, I stood up, "walked" him to the door, and said goodbye.

Of all the counseling, praying, and journaling, this one practice cleansed my system of the powerful hold I had allowed him to have on me. I left that vacation ready for a new life.

Ask!

There's one more point that I believe we women have a major weakness with: Asking for help, and then allowing ourselves to receive what others want to do for us.

Here's a great story that describes asking beautifully. We were preparing for the Marshall's Salon Services educational event in beautiful Lake Geneva, Wisconsin. The leaves on the trees outside the model room were already dressed in their fall colors, and inside the room, hair was being changed by design and color to demonstrate the new looks for the season.

For the third year in a row she arrived at model call, hoping that this time she'd be chosen for the makeover segment. One by one, she saw the other women being interviewed, asked to wait for further instructions, or dismissed and thanked for coming. She knew that feeling, and this year she didn't want to hear those familiar words, "Thank you for coming, but we're looking for a specific hair type in order to show the new looks."

"Please pick me, oh please pick me," she thought.

Finally the selection process was complete. Gary Harlan, the REDKEN National Performing Artist, was leaving the room and he looked her way. Still planted in her chair, he asked her if he could help her with anything.

"I've come here for three years in a row and each time I've been sent away. I really want a new look," she said shyly.

Gary took a look into her face. "Pretty," he thought. Although his initial impression of her hair was that it wasn't one he'd use for his presentation, he wanted so much just to do her hair and send her away. "I'll just do it as a gift," he thought. Little did he know that he was about to reorient her cells. With this one opportunity, he was going to make a difference in her life.

He had a Polaroid photo taken of her "before" look and posted it on the signed model release form.

She was ushered into the model room, where her hair was prepped for hair color. "Red," Gary thought, and he began to mix a formula that would bring out the best of her skin tone and eyes.

With her hair still wet from the color process, she was then led to Gary's partner, Flint Cross, who began to design her signature style. Letting go of length and weight, her hair began to respond to his shears. He was inspired, and she was thrilled. The final stops after blowdrying and styling were the makeup chair and wardrobe. The look came together so beautifully that Gary and Flint decided to put her on stage with them as their finale model.

Being presented to the audience was a dream come true for her. They were shown the "before" photo on large video screens. A collective gasp and thunderous applause filled the room when she walked from behind the stage and down the runway. She stood and allowed herself to absorb the adulation. This was finally her moment.

In the model room following the event, she thanked Gary and Flint with big hugs. Tears filled her eyes as she began to speak through the lump in her throat. "I've never felt, nor have I ever been told, that I was beautiful. Now I know that I am," she said. "I've been doing research in the last few months about women who are serving time in jail for killing their abusive husbands. I've been in an abusive situation for years and was seriously considering it. Now I realize I don't have to kill him; I just have to leave him. You've given me the courage to know that I can!"

Gary and Flint, just doing what they'd been doing weekend after weekend across the country, preparing for another educational event for salon professionals, took the time to care for a woman whose life could have taken a completely different course except that she was determined to ask for their help, allowed herself to receive their gifts of making her look and feel beautiful, and ultimately was free to live in her new beauty.

In the coming hours, I will be circumstantially aware of the opportunities I have to ask for someone's help. I'll break through my barriers of asking and be open to their own privilege of asking me for my help. As in this story from my visit a few years ago to South Africa.

"Do you know Oprah?" These were the first words Glendah spoke the minute she recognized my American accent and surmised that I was visiting Johannesburg on a business trip.

We were registered at Caesar's Hotel and Casino, the South African version of Caesar's Palace in Las Vegas. Our REDKEN team had invited leading salons from all over the country to join us for a two-day educational event, and I was privileged to be one of the guest speakers.

Walking each day from the hotel to the convention area, we'd pass through the array of shops and restaurants along the way. Glendah was the hostess at one of the more popular restaurants. My colleague Debbie Miller and I stopped in for tea that first afternoon. It was then that she asked the question, "Do you know Oprah?"

Although I confessed I didn't, I asked her what Oprah represented to her, a twenty-something, bright, vivacious South African girl. "She's my idol," she said. "She's just so wonderful, and one day I'll come to America so I can meet her."

Each day during our stay, I visited with Glendah as she would stand at the restaurant podium out in the passageway. We had our picture taken together, and I handed my business card to her with these words, "If I can ever do anything for you to help your dream come true to meet Oprah, please let me know." Upon my return to the States, I mailed her the photo with an encouraging word to follow her bliss. I asked her to stay in touch with me.

Within two weeks I received a phone call. Glendah spoke, "You told me to call you if you could help me in any way."

"Yes," I said. "Did you think of something I could help

you with?"

"Oh yes!" I could tell she was excited. "I want to go to college."

College! I thought, Oh no! She wants to go to college, and she's going to ask me to send her. I probed. "Where do you want to go to college?"

"I want to be an airplane mechanic, and I found a college here in Johannesburg, Kempton College, that has a two-year program and I wanted to ask you to help me go to college."

I drew a long, slow deep breath. "Glendah, you have a wonderful dream, and I'd love to help you become the best airplane mechanic. Tell me, do you know what the tuition is for such a school?"

"Yes, I already got all the information," she said in that beautiful South African accent reminding me of Meryl Streep in her role in Out of Africa, my favorite movie of all time.

"It's very expensive," she continued.

I gulped and braced myself for the worst.

"The tuition for the year is 3,600 Rand."

I quickly calculated on the latest exchange rate at the time, 9 rand to the dollar; this would be $400.00 US. Four hundred dollars, I thought. This is such a small investment for such a great return. I quickly said, "Yes, I'll do it. I'll believe in you and your dream, and I'll be happy to send you to Kempton College so you can become an airplane mechanic."

She organized her housing and enrolled in the college. I coordinated wiring the payment to her bank account, and coordinated her registrations through e-mails, phone calls, and faxes to the registrar. The total for her entire year's expenses was a rousing $1,000.00 US.

When I visited my bank to transfer the funds to the South African bank, I was overjoyed to be able to help a young woman in another country realize her dream. All the paperwork was complete. The funds were drawn from my account. I looked at the teller at my JP Morgan Chase Bank—where the right relationship is everything—and said, "Do you know what we just did?"

She looked at me puzzled, still focused on stamping "paid" on the transfer paperwork. "What did we just do?"

"We just helped a girl in South Africa go to college!" I was thrilled. Tears filled my eyes.

"We did?" she asked, with a satisfied smile and glistening eyes, too.

Traveling back to Johannesburg one year later, I was determined to visit with Glendah and see the college she was now calling home. I phoned her cell and received her voice message, and when I told her where I was staying I knew it was within a few short miles. Hopefully we'd be able to make a plan to get together.

Two days passed. No word. I was getting anxious that something had happened to her. It wasn't like her not to call. I was finishing a morning of R and R in the hotel spa, and as I was checking out, the reception phone rang and the receptionist handed the phone to me. This is strange, I thought, who knows I'm here? On the other end of the line was one of my colleagues saying they'd been looking for me because my friend Glendah was at the hotel and had been wandering around for an hour or more looking for me. We finally connected.

We hugged and cried. She introduced me to her aunt and uncle, who'd driven her to meet me. Then I invited her to lunch with me in the swank hotel restaurant. This is where the story got better for me. We were seated at a table with a view of the verandah, a beautiful fountain, a manicured lawn, and a swimming pool within our vision. We looked at the menu and ordered our lunch choices, and the breadbasket arrived with a variety of sumptuous breads and rolls. Soon enough, her spaghetti with meat sauce and my Caesar's salad with chicken arrived, and we dove into the delicious conversation and the food.

She revealed that she came from a village in the Kruger National Park and was one of four children, all who were privileged to graduate from high school. Her father was killed in an auto accident, and her mother was currently taking care of Glendah's three-year-old daughter, Crystal, while she was in Johannesburg getting her education. While she had been working at the restaurant where I met her a year ago, she would send money back to her mother to help in supporting Crystal. However, since she was going to school full-time, the money was no longer available. I could hardly stand to think that these precious people were destitute.

"How do they live now?" I asked. She assured me about her mother raising vegetables, peanuts, and maize, and that's what they eat. Her determination to finish her schooling now was making more sense. She wanted to provide for her loved ones.

"Why airline mechanics' school?" I asked her. She could've chosen any field, including my own, cosmetology.

She took a moment to answer. "It's not so much that I want to work on airplanes. It's that I care so much for people, and I want to make sure that when they fly on the airplanes that I work on, they will be completely safe." She continued, "There's a point at liftoff and landing that is very, very dangerous. It's called the 'angle of attack.' This is the place where the aircraft is between making the commitment to the higher altitude and the earth's gravity. The hydraulics must work perfectly at the 'angle of attack.' That's what I want to do; I want to be a hydraulic expert."

Although I was trying to eat my lunch during this conversation, I found my mouth was open only to gasp at her compassion and wisdom.

We ordered dessert. She wanted the tricolor gelato, and we both decided to go for it. More than once, she commented that she couldn't believe she was eating in such a beautiful place.

The check arrived. As I was taking care of it, I saw her eyeing the breadbasket, still on the table, untouched. "Did you pay for that?" she asked.

"Yes, when you ordered your meal, the bread was included in the price. Do you want to take it with you?"

"Oh, could I? I would have one of those pieces of bread, or rolls, for breakfast each morning."

My heart sank. How many times have I dined in beautiful places and left the bread on the table? How often have I prayed the line in the Lord's Prayer, "Give us this day our daily bread," and not given thanks for His provision every single day? Here was this special girl who was teaching me so much about appreciation of what's in front of us, not taking it for granted, and using what we've been given.

We took a car to the college campus and walked through the buildings, met the administrators, and took pictures galore. She was proud to show it off; I was prouder to watch her in her element.

Glendah's story continues to inspire. Her grades from the first year at Kempton College were more than acceptable. She passed with flying colors and was accepted to Denel Aviation Training Academy to continue her education. After two years of my sponsorship, it was time for her to find a local company that would offer an internship with the possibility of employment on the completion of her degree. Glendah's resourcefulness found a company, SAFAIR, a South African air freight company, and the person to plead her case to, Paul van Wyk.

I was willing to write the letter of recommendation. Knowing what I had learned of her, she would continue to make a model student and carry that ethic into her work life. I composed the letter and sent it via e-mail to Johannesburg on a Monday morning. By that afternoon, I received a response from Mr. van Wyk. He had made a point to go to Denel Academy in a suburb of Johannesburg, that afternoon, find Glendah, and have an initial interview with her. He was so impressed by her and by her story that although he didn't promise on the spot that she would be accepted into the intern program, he gave her a strong invitation to apply at the end of the school term.

In late September of her second year, she again met with Mr. van Wyk and a colleague for her official interview. They had prepared focused and difficult questions strictly about airline structure—her field of study. She was able to answer each question without hesitation. They were impressed.

"Why do you believe they were impressed with you?" I asked on the celebratory phone call from New York.

"Because I was prepared, studied hard, and knew all the

answers." This was a confident and accomplished girl. She knew it. Her voice reflected it.

They gave her an original date of January 2005 to begin her final internship. After a third interview, they found an opening in the fall of 2004—they couldn't wait to enroll her in their program. She found an apartment in close proximity to SAFAIR where she felt safe and could walk to work.

"Pass it on" is what I admonished her when we started this venture. "Whatever you've received from me, please promise that you'll pass it on. Begin with your daughter and make sure she gets her education."

She promised and eventually brought her young daughter to live with her. "It's important that she learn to speak English, so I'm sending her to school," she said.

When she returned to her home village one Sunday morning, she stood in front of the congregation: a big city girl now, realizing her dream, thanking God for the American woman who said "yes" to her request. She made an appeal to the other young people sitting there in amazement, faces with loss of hope written all over them. Glendah was adamant in her appeal. "Keep praying, keep believing, keep your dream alive. It can happen for you, too!"

Glendah will complete her internship with SAFAIR, earning her degree. I'll definitely go to Johannesburg for her graduation and be as proud of her as if she were my daughter as she walks across the stage to receive her diploma.

There's zero doubt that one day Glendah will make the seventeen-hour trip from South Africa to Chicago and realize her dream of meeting Oprah.

And it all came about as a result of the courage to *ASK*.

And Receive

When others offer to do an act of kindness for me, I'll allow myself to receive what it is they want to give to me.

It was a typical Southern California evening except for the fact that my parents were visiting from Ohio and I needed to run to the store to pick up our favorite evening snacks: popcorn, apples, and Pepsi. It may not seem like the healthiest of munchies, but in our home growing up it meant that we were all together sharing a television show, rooting for our favorite team, or playing a board game. I was thrilled to revisit those memories lodged in my taste buds.

I pulled up in the parking space at the closest convenience store near my home. Stepping from my car, I took a look at the dings and dents that had occurred in the five years since I'd driven it new off the lot. The damage was done in and around the Los Angeles airport, around the shopping malls, and in the office parking lot. The radio was on the blink. The cruise control was no longer cruising. I was beginning to be ashamed of pulling up to any valet parking attendant because, as you may know, in Los Angeles you are what you drive.

I was thinking to myself, what am I doing driving this pile of junk? This car isn't worthy of me! Then I saw him sitting with his back against the outside wall of the store, and he was holding a money cup in his hand.

"Nice car you got there, lady."

"Nice car?" I reacted, disbelieving what I had just heard. Then I found myself caught in a moment of gratitude. He was right. All in all, it was a nice car. It was faithful to get me to and from my home to destinations on those unpredictable freeways surrounding Los Angeles; it was cool in the summer and warm in the winter; and it was paid for in full, which meant I had no monthly obligation except to keep the vitals checked and the tank filled. I turned to this wise and generous man who sat begging for change and simply said, "Thanks. I do have a nice car."

Additionally to receiving, I will offer assistance to someone. If they refuse my offer, I will gently ask them to pause, "replay" the scene, and allow themselves to accept my offer of help. This will help them break through, too.

Asking and receiving. Two of the admonitions of the Master. And yet we are so reluctant to experience them. We must begin to allow others to do for us, and receive their gifts. Otherwise, we will die.

Hold On

Hold onto your goal, don't let go of your dream
Begin to believe that you are who you seem
Experience the moment
Trust the here and now
Cherish all the time spent
For it teaches you somehow to
Reach for the highest, allow only the best
Never be biased, move ahead of all the rest
Express every feeling, spend some time alone,
And you'll realize the beauty in yourself, your family
your home

- **Hold onto your goal, don't let go of your dream.**
  Simple to write or say; more challenging to
  actually do. Revisit the exercise in Chapter Two,
  "GLOWpoint one—your body," where you look

into a mirror and ask the questions "What can I do for you?" "Who can I get to assist me with doing this for you?" and "When do you want me to start doing this for you?" Once you have the courage to ask and are willing to hear the answer that comes from within you, you can begin to hold onto your dream because it came straight from you and no one else. What if it sounds preposterous, out of the question, or impossible? Hold on anyway.

- **Begin to believe that you are who you seem.** I call it "as-if-ing," or living as if it already is. Begin to believe you are being, doing, and having what your inner self has revealed, and it will be just a matter of moments, hours, or days before the evidence makes itself appear.

- **Experience the moment, trust the here and now.** This is the secret of all time. To be as-if-ing is to allow ourselves the luxury of truly being in the moment. I call it the precious present. I relinquish the regrets of the past and allow the outcomes of tomorrow to be assured due to my concentration on the people, events, and opportunities of today. Trust that where you are and what you're doing are exactly where you supposed are to be, and whatever is happening is the best thing that could've ever happened. What we are responsible for is the effort we make to take care of ourselves, to do exactly what we can do every moment to serve and take care of others, so there is no room for resentment. When we are accountable to the best of our effort, with love, we can release the outcome to God and rest assured that the best thing will occur. When we try to control the outcome, we're playing God and that's not our role. Trust where you are—here and now—and experience the rest and release that comes with it.

- **Cherish all the time spent, for it teaches you somehow.** Have you ever looked in a dictionary for the word "cherish"? It is a beautiful word that we don't use often. It means to "hold dear with respect": To respect the time of your life and exchange it only for the people and events that support the goal and dream that you established when you looked into the mirror. Remember? If your time is being spent with those who would rob the goal or splash negativity all over your dream, they may need to be excused from your life. I've learned that not everyone needs to be in my world. Nor do I need to be in everyone else's. Those who I choose to bring into my inner circle and share my goals and dreams with are those who help me cherish them. Time spent with them is thrilling and beneficial for us both.

- **Reach for the highest, allow only the best.** What is the highest and best for you? Highest and best in what area? Maybe you'll want to take an inventory of the Five GLOWpoints: your body, your thoughts, your relationships, your resources, and your service. Can you define the highest and best expression of yourself in each of those areas?

- **Never be biased, move ahead of all the rest.**
Holding onto prejudices, bigotry, or biases is
not a reflection on anyone other than you. It
proves your restrictive fear of allowing others
their rightful place in the world and your life.
Each criticism you express is actually a criticism of
yourself, for what you see in others, good or bad,
is what you see within: Otherwise, you'd never
recognize it. Forsaking judgment by saying silently
to yourself, "And I am that too," will set you free
from others' judgments of you. The world is full
of people who are consumed with worry that
someone else will take what is rightfully theirs,
and so their line of defense is to express their
fear through criticism, cynicism, and bias against
the person. You need never be concerned that
someone is ahead of you or better off than you,
or getting the credit or accolades you deserve.
No one, *no one*, can withhold your spiritual good
from you. What is yours to experience is there
for your recognition and acceptance, and you can
move ahead with confidence.

- **Express every feeling.** If it's your feeling, it's real
and it's yours! I've found that feelings "come to
pass," which means they don't last very long—
both good ones and not so good ones. However,
I've also come to realize that when I have a feeling
that is aching to be expressed, I have choices about
what to do with it. I can:

- express my feelings immediately and accept the response and consequences.
- share my feelings with my friends and hope to solicit their support that feeds my self-pity or ego.
- go "underground" and either celebrate the good feeling alone or, in the case of a not-so-good feeling, allow its negative effect to fester in my mind and heart.

Expressing the feeling and its effect to the person in an honest way with loving overtones will result in closer communication and strengthened bonds. The important issue is to be willing to express and relinquish control of the outcome.

• **Spend some time alone.** "Alone" is a beautiful word. Behind the word is the ability to be with yourself and be content with your values, which lead to thoughts, which lead to words, which lead to actions, which lead to outcomes. Constantly needing the company of other people, their input, and their demands is an ultimate drain and can deplete the reserves. Being alone can bring a sense of relaxation and can open the ears of your heart to the still small voice that is constantly aching to be heard. With people around all the time, phones ringing, and computer messages glaring against a lighted screen, that voice is drowned out. Spending time alone may be uncomfortable for some at first. It may require short spans of time to get used to it. Then expanding the time on a daily and weekly basis will give inner strength for the outer world as you learn to put your trust in yourself being alone. You'll come to see you really aren't alone at all.

- **You'll realize the beauty of yourself, your family, and your home.** True beauty is to see the beauty in those you live with, in the place you call home. Home is a beauty-full place when it provides four basic qualities of beauty: generosity, hospitality, forgiveness, and gratitude. When our home surrounds us with these four values, we'll emerge each day to meet our world with those values in our hearts, and beauty will surround every step we take, every word we speak. We'll be an active contributor to God's work, creating beautiful experiences based on these four values. We are here to create beauty wherever we serve, and we can begin serving those at home.

NOTES ON MY GLOWING RELATIONSHIPS

Glow Question: Where do my deep gladness and the world's great hunger meet? The surrendered Self is the secret to life. Listen attentively, care deeply, and love profoundly.

5

GLOWpoint four—your resources

"Bring all the tithes into the storehouse so there will be enough food in my Temple. If you do, says the Lord Almighty, I will open the windows of Heaven. I will pour out a blessing so great you won't have enough room to take it in! Try it! Let me prove it to you!"—Malachi 3:10

Because this promise is true, what could possibly be stopping us from giving? I'm not talking about giving everything away to others. I'm fundamentally talking about taking care of myself by trusting that when I give the first 10 percent (yes, that's 10 percent) of my income to advancing spiritual good for others, my needs will be taken care of in abundant ways. Some say, "The truly intelligent ones are those who are generous."

Before I pay anyone else, I invest this as a statement of faith and loyalty to the One from whom I receive all creative, productive ideas—the ideas that turn into my income. I don't have to be afraid that if I give I'll run out. I'll always have enough to meet my needs.

I once subscribed to the theory that if you have an income of 100 percent and commit 10 percent, you're forced to live on the remaining 90 percent. This was the "story" I told myself until along came Mark Victor Hansen and Robert G. Allen and their band of Enlightened Millionaires, who showed me a new way in their best-selling book, *The One Minute Millionaire*.

When you tithe 10 percent, rather than being a "subtractor" it becomes a "multiplier" so that you no longer live on the remaining 90 percent but are abundantly blessed with 1,000 percent to put toward good works, great experiences, and expanded learning.

God doesn't know the meaning of poverty. When I am dealing with God, I am dealing with first-class things.

When I read this for the first time, I was stunned and filled with joy. Each time I've shared it with my family and friends, the same reaction takes place. It's the truth. And it will work for you, too! For more information on Enlightened Millionaires and *The One Minute Millionaire*, log onto www.markvictorhansen.com.

By getting honest about the emotional hold that money has and admitting exactly where you are financially, you can begin to get honest with all other relationships and situations in your life. Why not commit to that kind of naked honesty beginning now?

What is the gross income printed on your paycheck? If you don't receive a paycheck and are being paid in other forms, calculate your gross monthly income and write it in this space.

$\underline{\hspace{2cm}}

What is 10 percent of that number?

$\underline{\hspace{2cm}}

This is your tithing amount. Remember, it's a multiplier! Not a subtractor!

Talk about an investment that's more sure and secure than anything Wall Street could promise. This is guaranteed. The equivalent may not come back directly in cash. It will come back in a variety of ways: in health, in ideas, in savings, in gifts, in being taken out for dinner, in being invited to stay in a friend's vacation home. You'll know when you're being gifted for the gift you gave.

And the most important thing to remember when it's happening is to acknowledge where it's coming from (the real source), accept it graciously, and be grateful.

Investing in My "Me Fund"

Next, acknowledge your worth and reward it. Do this by setting an amount aside as a "Me Fund." It may be a savings account; it may be a private cash stash in a simple jar. How much you put into your "Me Fund" may vary. As you become accustomed to doing it, genuinely recognize your worth and reward yourself.

Think of it as an evolution. At one time in your earning, you may have allowed yourself to acquire those things that you needed, then you progressed to those things you wanted, and now it's time to graduate to investing in those things you deserve.

The "Me Fund" accumulates to provide you with purchasing power for some material goal, for a meaningful experience, or to help you achieve long-term security. This leads again to greater future giving power!

Ask yourself: What is it I truly believe I deserve and am willing to have for myself?

Managing Your Income

Financial challenges may not result from inadequate income; they often result from inadequate income management. When you learn to plan your earning, giving, investing, and spending, you'll realize the financial goals you've set.

Accepting responsibility for learning how to meet your financial obligations plays the major role in taking care of others and yourself.

Answer the following questions honestly:

- Do I have a consistent plan for financial giving?
- Do I consider myself my best investment and have a "Me Fund"?
- Do I have an adequate savings plan to cover my expenses should an emergency arise?
- Do I use credit cards too frequently and increase the cost of my purchases by paying high interest rates?
- Am I savvy in finding financial institutions that offer lower rates than I'm currently paying on those credit cards?

Before you can begin to plan for your financial future, you must understand where you are today. It's such a courageous feeling to "get naked" financially and truly admit what you earn, spend, invest, save, and charge. It's alarming how much money leaks easily through your fingers.

As you allow yourself to become vulnerable in the next experience, you must remember to stay with it. Being made accountable in black and white and seeing where you are will put you well on your way to securing your financial future.

Answer these basic questions and jot the answer next to each one.

What is my gross monthly income? $ _____

What is my net monthly income? $ _____

What are my basic monthly expenses?

Housing	$ _____
Home Insurance	$ _____
Property Taxes	$ _____
Food	$ _____
Medical/Prescriptions	$ _____
Health Insurance	$ _____
Car Payment	$ _____
Car Gas/Oil/Maintenance	$ _____
Car Insurance	$ _____
Car Taxes	$ _____
Phone	$ _____
Cable/Internet	$ _____
Utilities	$ _____
Clothing	$ _____

Professional Services	$ _____
Entertainment	$ _____
Other	$ _____
Credit Card Payments	$ _____

What is the total of these monthly expenses? $ _____

Subtract these expenses from your net income. $ _____

If your bottom line is zero or a minus figure, it's time to seriously take that first giant leap of faith and give 10 percent where it can bless and be blessed. It's the first sure step to financial discipline and balance. Don't give because *have* to; give because you *get* to.

As generosity is expressed to you, you'll begin to receive and recognize it as a gift and immediately be grateful. The more grateful you are, the more you'll have to be grateful for. The real deal is to be willing to neither limit what you can gain nor limit what you can lose.

All the money you'll ever earn comes through other people. Aligning your relationships is vital to your financial security.

Here's a story that demonstrates the point.

REDKEN Australia sponsored a great moment of growth for me. I was invited to train the Aussie sales and education team and to meet our leading salon professionals in the "land down under." This dynamic team was brought together at the exclusive Opal Cove Resort on the Eastern shore.

Among the group were Bennie and Tracey Tognini of Brisbane. One evening they offered to give me a makeover. They arrived at my hotel room armed with all the tools of their trade that made them award-winning designers in hair and makeup. As Bennie began cutting my hair, I said to Tracey,

"I just wish I could get rich doing what I do." She looked around the beautifully appointed suite, through the plate glass windows overlooking the aquamarine water. Then she proceeded to teach me a lesson I'll never forget.

"Now, what would you do if you were rich?" she asked. "You'd travel around the world, stay in first-class hotels, and have people tending to your every need. Wake up, Ann. This is rich!"

And so it was.

Yes, through REDKEN I've been blessed with being granted the opportunities of seeing all of the places in the world I've ever wanted to see. Boarding airplanes in major cities, I look at the travel posters covering the walls of jet ways and say to myself as I pass them, one by one, "I've been there, I've stayed there, I've eaten there." And I always remember to be thankful.

From now on, I'll be aware of those rich moments that provide me with the experiences to look, feel, sound, smell, and taste what rich is.

How about you? Take a moment and define what "rich" is to you by using your five senses.

- How does rich look?
- How does rich feel?
- How does rich sound?
- How does rich smell?
- How does rich taste?

What you'll find is that you are rich already! And with your managed financial plan, your money will be there to verify it.

Traveling to my sister Jan's home for Thanksgiving one year, I noticed a bulletin board outside the United Methodist Church in the small Ohio town of Sunbury. I read the words "A Grateful Mind Is a Great Mind." Great thought for Thanksgiving; great thought for today!

A lifelong friend, Paul Franklin, called one December to tell me he had been contemplating closing the doors of his film production business. He started his company over twenty-five years ago and had steady positive growth investing in people, equipment, and locations. Then, with the unfortunate turn of events with the economy and employees, he began to see the morale and competency of his business coming unraveled. He was at the brink when an employee recommended that he read the *New York Times* bestseller *The Prayer of Jabez*, written by Bruce Wilkinson. (Find out more about it at www.prayerofjabez.com.)

Everyday for thirty days, Paul made the *Prayer* his prayer.

"Oh that You would bless me indeed,
and enlarge my territory,
that Your hand would be with me,
and that You would keep me from evil,
that I may not cause pain!"—1 Chronicles 4:9–10

He prayed with sincerity, with humility. It was just a matter of time before the phones began ringing off the hook and business was—in his words—"coming out of the woodwork." He recommended that I read the book and begin practicing the same daily ritual.

In January, I began. Day by day, I've been faithful in my morning quiet time to repeat the prayer and affirm it as my truth. It was in the area of "enlarging my territory" that I began to see and feel the effects.

Modern Salon Magazine, the leading trade magazine in the United States, asked that I write a biweekly column on their website entitled "Spirit Moves"; the American Beauty Association voted unanimously to appoint me as the chairperson for their annual charity ball; and David Craggs, the president of the professional division of L'Oreal USA enlisted *me to head a newsletter targeted to the 1,000-plus employees of the division.* In addition, *Hair Color and Design* magazine publisher Bob Lupinacci gave me the opportunity to write a bimonthly column entitled "Human Spirit."

These and many other "territory expansion" opportunities have come my way, such as speaking opportunities in industries outside of the professional salon business. One of the most rewarding was being named director of health, beauty, and spirit for Shape Your Life destination resort programs. SYL offers extraordinary programs and events focusing on enhancing sense of self, community living, and spiritual evolution. We've received testimonials stating, "You not only shape bodies; you shape souls." For information, see www.shapeyourlife.tv.

In October 2002 I was invited to be one of 500 spiritual and religious, business, and governmental women to attend the first-ever Women's Global Peace Initiative at the United Nations in Geneva, Switzerland. As one of the speakers in the business section of this meeting, I focused my comments on "The Beauty of Peace and the Peace of Beauty," encouraging women from every creed, color, and race attending to take time for themselves in an act of love and care. Out of that conference, the Business Council for Peace was created with a handful of businesswomen in New York City. The outreach is to find markets for the exquisite products produced by women in conflict and postconflict areas of the world—specifically, Rwanda, Afghanistan, and the Middle East. It's thrilling to watch courage increase as confidence in economic security increases. For more information, see www.bpeace.com.

I began to realize that expanding my territory also meant expanding my capacity. I relied on the Spirit's still small voice within to guide me in the areas where I have no expertise such as fund-raising.

Accolades came, too: The North American Hairstyling Awards Hall of Leaders award, the New York Women's Agenda "Star" Award, and the Coalition of Christian Colleges and Universities' recognition in their publication as an outstanding alumna, alongside my classmate, Brad Moore, president of Hallmark Productions.

In the summer of 2004, I was honored as the recipient of the Spirit of Life award designated to an industry leader by City of Hope. I recall the day I received the call congratulating me on the honor: I also received a call from my mother informing me that my little sister, Cathy, had discovered a malignant lump on her right breast. The Hope for her came from the successful research conducted at the City of Hope. This for me was the greatest honor, which completed our industry's Triple Crown recognition.

We completed the "Hope and the City" campaign with a record-making $1,400,000 raised for breast cancer research.

The Prayer of Jabez is written on a small card, which is in my daily meditation book so I remember to pray it. A friend of mine has his on his bathroom shelf, which reminds him to pray it as he shaves each morning. Copy it down, put it somewhere you'll see it daily, and watch the miracles begin to happen.

Dreams

Goals and dreams and plans and schemes
Trying to get my share
Of life and love
And wealth
I shove
And in shoving I get nowhere
But if I pause and just be stilled
I realize my dreams are being fulfilled
So I can rest in peace
And give such a sigh of release
For all my hopes and dreams I find
Are really already mine
They're already mine
When I've pictured them in
My mind

- **Goals and dreams and plans and schemes.** Write them down, affirm them "as if" they were already yours, check off the steps you've made toward manifesting, and believe it will lead to one supreme result.
- **Trying to get my share of life and love and wealth.** Trying means striving, struggling, grasping, and clutching after your share.
- **I shove.** You shove, afraid that someone else will get (or take) what is rightfully yours, or afraid that if you don't strive with enough gusto, using all your energy and talent, you may pass from this earth

never having known or realized your full potential of accumulation/achievement, so you shove your way into opportunities, others' lives, and events.

- **And in shoving I get nowhere.** It's a natural law that what you resist persists. What you push against pushes against you. What you think you're doing to assist in the good of your life is actually working against you!

- **But if I pause and just be stilled.** Now here's a concept that has begun to hit mainstream. But has it hit with impact on your life? "Pause and be stilled" is an action that invites graciousness in, invites your "share" in, allows for the space it needs to occupy your life, and brings with it the love and energy it needs to sustain it. "Be still and know," admonishes the scriptures. "Pause and be stilled" works!

- **I realize my dreams are being fulfilled.** As you rest in Divine timing, every good and perfect gift is allowed to manifest. You have all these when you "be" all that *you* are. When your dreams come from Divine inspiration within you, and you begin "being" the character that can handle the very thing you are dreaming of, then only God's intervention would stop you from having it. Because He gave the dream in the first place, there's no reason to stop it from coming in all its fullness.

- **So I can rest in peace.** Let go! Be happy!

- **And give such a sigh of release.** Literally breathing in deeply and opening your mouth to sigh out is a demonstration of letting go. As you do, resign not only to the big "whatever," but also to the big "whenever."

- **For all my hopes and dreams I find are really already mine.** They're already mine, when I've pictured them in my mind. When you visualize, in detail, the outcome you desire in alignment with your values, then all your thoughts, words, and actions galvanize around that vision. You become a human magnet drawing to you the people and opportunities to make that vision a reality.

If you've been able to picture each of these areas of your life, then it proves they already exist. What do you need to *be* to *have* these things you want to bring into your life? Simply begin "being" that. Your goals and dreams and plans and schemes will be given to you in the right timing.

Think of it. Even if those dreams in the movie of your mind never made it to the physical realm, oh what joy they're brought you as you visualized them. I've found that what counts most is what I've become in the process of my dreams unfolding.

NOTES ON MY GLOWING RESOURCES

Glow Question: Is my giving motivated by Love? The distance of my love is the distance of my giving. The focus now is giving rather than receiving.

6

GLOWpoint five—your service

"For God did not give us a spirit of timidity, but a spirit of power, of love and of self-discipline."—II Timothy 1:7

This GLOWpoint is the beginning and the end. Without God's Spirit, the source of loving kindness and passion, compassion and empathy, and patience and surrender, none of the other points can or will glow at their authentic brilliance. This is the seat of acceptance of *self* and others in this present moment.

We make time for the things that we value most. What would someone learn about me if they followed me around for three months? My values—not my habits—form the basis that becomes the routines of my life.

Housed here, too, are the two major life issues that can propel us to thrive. They are forgiveness and gratitude.

Forgiveness Is Everything

The unforgiving attitude is about being stuck in the past. Past hurts, past betrayals, past disappointments, past mistakes, past misjudgments, past affairs. Past . . . past . . . past . . . past . . . past.

Guess what! The past is passed. Don't go there.

Grief is housed in the past. And as long as you choose to dwell there, you're not here. And if you're not here, you're grieving and missing what is happening, who is speaking, what feelings are aroused, and what learning can be accomplished. Grief is felt in the heart, and the heart is affected. It's no wonder that coronary disease is on the rise, since the heart muscle and the energy that feeds it are trying to exist on the morsels that are thrown to it by the memories of what *was* rather than the fresh happenings of what *is*.

Unrequited grief leads to dis-ease and, for many, death. And even those who are alive are actually dead in the moment.

So, to the point of forgiveness: Just do it. Do it now. Do it forever. Do it in the moment you feel the need to do it. Do it for what's been grieving you for years, months, days, and minutes. Write a "Dear Whomever" forgiveness letter to the one who you believe you need to forgive, or who you'd like to ask for forgiveness. You don't have to send it. It's not about them. It's about you and your willingness to ask or grant forgiveness. They never have to know you wrote it. But you do. And the minute you write it, you'll feel the release of the load that it has kept you under. Like a runner trying to complete the New York Marathon with ten-pound sandbags on his or her legs, so does not forgiving bog you down with unnecessary burdens. Run free!

This issue of being burdened reminds me of a traveling story. I was delivered to the American Airlines terminal at JFK airport in New York. Since I was going to be traveling for nearly three weeks to faraway places such as Seoul, Taiwan, Tokyo, Montreal, and Nice, I loaded my three bags with everything I thought I would need for any situation in which I would find myself.

Because of serious construction around the airport, it became apparent that I would have to roll my bags into the terminal and find an agent who could check me in. I must have looked obviously weighed down and troubled when a skycap approached me with an empty luggage cart and a big smile. "Do you need some help?" he asked.

I looked at him as if to say, "Yeah sure, now you show up," because I had already made it through the construction maze to the inside where within a few steps I'd be at the Business Class check-in counter.

He gave me one more "Huh? May I help you?"

I was still holding my heavy load, feeling the handles of my bags cutting my palms.

"All you have to do is just say the word," he said.

I said, "Yes."

He went into action. In a moment the load was lifted, and I was all checked in.

This illustrates what the Spirit is saying to me everyday: "Just say the word and I'll take your load, your weights, your pain."

For me, sometimes, being stuck with the pain is more comfortable than the temporary pain of the "shift" that would lead to pleasure.

The release of unnecessary weight is exactly what I believe happens when we forgive or ask for forgiveness. Sometimes all it takes is the willingness to write the note. It's serious stuff. You can do it. Begin like this:

Dear _____,

I forgive you completely for what you did to me.
(Or) I want you to forgive me completely for what I
did to you.

You can go into further detail if you need to purge deeply. Go
ahead. Anguish, cry, get angry, stop writing, and start again.
Whatever it takes. But write until your hand stops. You'll know
you're finished. And you can begin to live.

It's no wonder why Jesus asked in the Lord's Prayer to
"forgive us our debts as we forgive our debtors," and why
the last words he spoke before he took his last breath were
"Father, forgive them . . ." He knew that physical, emotional, and
spiritual health—and, yes, eternal rewards—result from the act
of forgiveness. Life begins with forgiveness.

A number of recent studies conducted at places like Stanford
University and Duke University have showed that there is
evidence of emotional and physical health payoffs from the
act of forgiveness. One from Duke demonstrated that among
those who have chronic back pain, those who have practiced
forgiveness experience lower levels of pain and less associated
psychological problems like anger and depression than those
who have not forgiven.

After forgiveness comes gratitude. Life thrives on gratitude.

How Can I Say "Thanks"?
Earlier, in the fourth GLOWpoint, you read about being grateful
for the gifts that come as the results of giving. We spoke of being
grateful for people and telling them so. Now it's time to express
your gratitude. Remember: "I only have what I express."

Just as we wrote a letter of forgiveness, let's now compose a letter of thankfulness to someone who means so much to you. Someone who has been there for you. Someone who has gone to bat for you or been your advocate. Someone who's never passed judgment or been critical. Or someone who for the benefit of your own good was willing to take the risk and give you honest feedback.

You know who it is. This letter you may want to send. It will fill your heart and theirs. A bond will be set for life. You'll be able to count on each other even more deeply than before. Again, simply put your pen on the page and just begin to write.

Dear _____,
How can I say thanks for the things that you've done for me?

Then go into specifics on those memories or issues where you felt the supportive, guiding hand of your friend. It doesn't have to be long; it just has to be heartfelt. And they will feel you through the words on the page. Just as you would like to hear from someone you've done something special for, write to your special someone in the same tone, words, and feelings. They'll get it. And they'll never be the same.

In Chapter Two, the chapter on your body, I suggested a deep-breathing exercise of breathing in the word "joy" and breathing out the word "fear." Now, I want you to have another sensation.

Sit with your back pressed against the chair and your feet on the floor; relax your shoulders and face. Close your eyes. Take three cleansing breaths in through the heart and out through the solar plexus with these words: "Breathe in gratitude; breathe out forgiveness."

Check in with your body, mind, emotions, spirit. . . . How do you feel? Sit in this feeling until you absolutely have to move.

HeartMath LLC, a highly researched scientific approach to stress management and creativity, was introduced to me at the 2003 Spirit in Business conference in San Francisco. The originators of HeartMath showed quantitative results on the reduction of stress hormones by three short steps: Shift, Focus, and Sense.

First, shift your attention from the stressful influence to your heart and take several long, slow, deep breaths. This one action massages your heart and slows and steadies your heart rate variability, which affects your ability to think and communicate clearly.

Next, focus on generating a sincere, positive feeling of appreciation for someone, something, or somewhere in your life. This step balances the hormones cortisol and DHEA, which shifts the influx of the negative emotion to positive.

Third, sense the subtle shift in how you're perceiving the stressful situation. A more effective and efficient action can now be taken to prolong the balanced feeling and contribute to a different outcome.

As a certified HeartMath trainer, I've seen with my own eyes an immediate shift in the salon professionals in the release and relief they experience through the breathing and gratitude they practice. It improves their ability to reduce stress in their work and in their lives. For more information about HeartMath, point your browser to www.HeartMath.com.

Write in your journal the ten things you have to be grateful for this moment. At the end of the day, ask yourself this question: "When were the times today when I felt grateful?"

I Will Rejoice and Be Glad

One Sunday morning, I was watching the *Hour of Power* broadcast from the Crystal Cathedral in Garden Grove, California. On many working Sundays, I've turned on my television in the hotel room and, while getting ready for a seminar or training session, I've worshipped in the beauty of the palm trees swaying in the backdrop of that architectural wonder of the world.

I've been there. I've heard the mighty pipe organ accompanying the choir's voices singing "Morning Has Broken." From my hotel room, I projected myself into the pew and looked into the eyes of the pastor as he greeted me.

Dr. Robert Schuller rose to the pulpit in his robe and colorful doctoral shawl to call us to worship. His familiar imploring words rang through that massive, glass-enclosed building: "This is the day the Lord has made. Let us rejoice and be glad in it."

If you've ever heard the exuberance of Dr. Schuller's voice and his distinct pronunciations, you'll understand when I tell you that I heard something new when he called me to worship that day. What I heard was this: "This is the day the Lord has made. Let us *rechoice* and be glad in it."

"*Rechoice.*" That's what it's all about. Daily, I have the ability and opportunity to rechoose the way that I live, the ways I give, the things I say. Just as the words across the bottom of the window shades at Saks Fifth Avenue remind me that the artisans are changing the mood and fashions on the mannequins inside and their work is indeed a "Work in Progress," so is my life. And the choices I make moment by moment, day by day, are creating the artwork that I'm putting my signature on for the world to see.

I don't let my past dictate who I am, but I let it be a part of who I will become. Dream large, pray large, receive large. I can imagine God saying to us, "I have no one except you to help me to realize my dream." This excites me to respond to God and say, "Yeah!"

Ninety percent of life is showing up. I don't know what's going to happen, but I know nothing's going to happen if I don't show up. With every breath I take, I have a choice to make.

Rechoice

In the morning all I hear are the birds and Your voice
Another day that You have made
Another chance to rechoice
Rechoice in the way that I live
Rechoice in the ways I can give
Rechoice everything that I say
Day
After
Day
After
Day
I have the choice.
Any wonder I awake with a "yes" on my mind
"yes" to loving
One another
And "yes" to be kind
Rechoice in the way that I live
Rechoice in the ways I can give
Rechoice everything that I say
Day
After
Day
After
Day
I have the choice.

Anything that makes me feel less than joyful is not coming from Love. I can, in the instant, make the choice to separate myself from anything that separates me from Love.

Loving Service Is a Gentle Thing

The salon environment, with its transformers of beauty who listen with a caring ear and offer a compassionate touch, is one of the last safe places on earth where Love is spoken and demonstrated. It is an atmosphere where miracles take place.

From the birth of a baby and his first haircut, through the first day of school, high school proms, college graduations, weddings, divorces, career transfers, and saying "goodbye" in death, salon professionals play a vital role in every life stage for their clients. No one else, except perhaps a church congregation, has the intimate knowledge of families and their life triumphs and traumas as the salon professional.

And so, in this atmosphere of Love, a client can feel safe to share highs, lows, sorrows, joys, achievements, failures, disappointments, losses, and gains. To listen to their innermost secrets and hold them in the process takes a special person in a special place. Love is a kingdom where things are turned upside down.

As a familiar phrase from the twelve-step program reminds us: "We are only as sick as our secrets." When salon clients feel safe to tell their innermost secrets, be gently touched in the process, and leave the experience looking more beautiful or handsome, they are not as sick as they were when they arrived. They have been healed.

I'm reminded of Dr. Ron DiSalvo, REDKEN's vice president of research and development on a seminar platform in 1975. It was my first educational event as a new field representative.

Ron was facing the group with his finger pointing out toward the future when he said, "In the 1990s hairdressers will be the doctors of the future."

The 1990s, I thought; that's eons away. And, yet, here we are in the new millennium and Ron was right. The Latin word for "doctor" is translated as "teacher." Certainly the salon professionals I've been privileged to know are teaching their clients about themselves in ways beyond the common haircut or hair color design.

Salon professionals including hair designers, hair colorists, nail technicians, estheticians, and massage therapists are offering healing touch and healing conversation with every person who steps into their healing environment. These "doctors" connect with people, interacting at their most vulnerable place and offer treatments and hope and counsel. They increase health by improving the quality of the client's life.

I've seen with my own eyes that when salon professionals are willing to surrender their talents and gifts to God, they begin to see their "job" turn into their "work." It becomes their mission to contribute to the spirit and the image of their clients. They rest in the knowledge that they'll be rewarded spiritually with Love that is never-ending and forever refreshing. As Saint Francis of Assisi prayed, "For it is in giving, that we receive."

People will clamor to the doors of those salons filled with balanced "Star Servers" to feel enclosed within their safe harbor. Today, more than ever, the salon will be needed for these purposes.

Willing to Be a Servant
Now we can proceed to do the work of healing gently through

serving humbly by glowing brightly. To begin the process, I want to focus on willingness to serve.

I didn't say "be a slave"; I said "to serve."

The privilege of serving is acknowledged in ancient scriptures as the first honor: "We must be the servants of all." Even the Master humbled himself to wash the feet of his friends. When the macho disciple Peter refused and declared, "You're not washing my feet!" Jesus replied, "If you don't allow me to wash your feet, you're not one of me."

Peter relented. "All right, my hands and my head as well."

At that moment, Jesus set up the first model of a full-service salon and the full-service servant. If that work was something he did to prove humility and generosity, it's certainly a great endorsement of what happens everyday in salons worldwide.

Service is the idea.

"Serve us" is the action.

To thrive in your service is a result of aligning your star's Five GLOWpoints.

Being willing to serve is an issue of the spirit and of clear and clean thoughts.

Being able to serve your pure relationships is the privilege of the bright body, which will result in being rewarded with bountiful resources.

Take a few minutes to ponder this thought.

Notes on My Glowing Service

Glow Questions: How abundant do I want to be? How fully can I serve? How fully can I be present to find a need and serve it?

7

all that you can be

On April 1, 1975, I packed my wardrobe into my 1973 Oldsmobile Cutlass, hitched on a U-Haul trailer filled with my earthly possessions, and drove away from my parent's home. Stopping in Kansas City on the way out to California, I dropped the trailer with a friend to care for my belongings as I made my way to my new life with REDKEN.

The hours on the road seemed to speed by as I made my way westward, stopping at an occasional roadside restaurant for a snack and a motel to rest my road-weary body.

All along my journey, I'd hand-carried that plaque that had hung on the kitchen wall of my grandparent's modest home. The original string my Grandma tied onto the hooks embedded in the back for hanging was still there.

I traveled mile after mile with the plaque on my dashboard,

and nightly carried it into my motel room as my protector until the morning light would appear. The raised letters spoke truth, reminding me "I can do all things through Christ which strengtheneth me."

Out somewhere in Arizona, I knew my journey was nearing its completion and in a few hours I'd be entering Los Angeles: My new life, new company, new adventure. My fears began to surface now, and as they mounted I knew of one sure action to take. Call home!

I pulled into the next rest stop, stretched my legs, made my way to a phone, and dialed collect. Faithful as always, my beautiful mother answered, "Good morning!" and I burst into tears.

"Mommy, I'm so scared. I don't know if I can do this. I don't know what to expect. It's bigger than I am; I'm just so scared."

In her quiet, reassuring way, she began to speak. "Honey, just get back in your car and keep driving. In thirty days you won't remember you even went through the desert."

I thanked her for being there, for sharing her wisdom. I got a Pepsi out of the machine and started back to my car. Sitting silently behind the wheel, I put the key into the ignition and the gearshift in reverse. My eyes glanced at the plaque that had accompanied me for nearly 2,500 miles. It read, "I can do all things through Christ which strengtheneth me."

I can do all things, I thought. Wait a minute: I can do all things . . . does that mean I can do anything?

The answer was a Divine "Of course!" I found myself driving with one hand, and with the other exploring the glove box for a pencil, pen, paper, and napkin—anything that I could use to capture what would be the first of several poems to be written through me. I'm offering it to you toward the end of our journey together, because it sums up and reinforces everything you can become when all Five GLOWpoints are aligned.

Anything

I can do anything
I can be a light that shines
I can help in every way
To open eyes of the blind
Listening to their problems
Will heal the wounds of time
Loving all about them
Will set free their minds

He will give strength each day
My faith won't have any bound
I can do anything
When I live on higher ground
A higher plane than I have found
Everything's on higher ground

I can have anything
Success will come through love and health
It will be for all to share
If not to give
What good is wealth
Watching lives make changes
Because of words I've spoken
Hopeful rearranges
For hearts that once were broken

What I have
I want to share
You'll never know, want, or need
I can have anything
With faith as big as one small seed

I can do
You can too
Anything
We'll have everything
With faith as big as one small seed

- **I can do anything.** Is this true? It is if the "anything" you're attempting to do is an idea, urge, or leading of the Spirit that gives you knowledge on how to accomplish something.
- **I can be a light that shines.** A brightness of Spirit can glow from behind your eyes and through your skin; it can float in your walk and percolate in your personality.
- **I can help in every way to open eyes of the blind.** When someone is lost in an issue, a challenge, or a problem, or is swirling in a whirlpool of dwindling self-esteem, they are blind to the possibilities of hope and renewal. You can be the one to open their eyes and give them new sight.
- **Listening to their problems will heal the wounds of time.** Just listening without judgment or advice, letting the other know they're heard by making eye-to-eye contact, nodding, and gently touching, can send healing waves through their body and Spirit. Whatever they've been carrying requires only three things to become merely a memory and no longer a burden: Climbing above the issue by seeing a bigger reason, confessing it, and continuing communication about it in your nonjudgmental presence until they feel released from its power.
- **Loving all about them will set free their minds.** Let your presence be a safe harbor. Loving others unconditionally, no matter what they've said, thought, or done, is a Divine gift, rare in the world. If we are only as sick as our secrets, and we confess

them openly to each other in a safe environment, when we leave each other we are healed of that which we have confessed and we are set free.

- **He will give strength each day.** The best part is, you don't have to muster up your own cleverness, energy, or power to be there for others. Just your willingness to show up will bring with it the strength from God you'll need to endure.
- **My faith won't have any bound.** Faith, the vision of things hoped for, has no limit when the vision has come from God. All things are possible because all things already are. You become the means, the instrument, used to make them manifest in your world.
- **I can do anything when I live on higher ground.** Living on higher ground begins with your thoughts—whatever is kind, true, loving, gracious, lovely, noble, and worthy of praise. Let your mind dwell here, and all that comes is a reflection of that and only that.
- **A higher plane than I have found, everything's on higher ground.** Even when we believe we're thinking the highest and best about a situation or person, we can go further. It's like when I'm in a yoga position and believe I've stretched to my limit, my instructor gently nudges me another inch or two. The limits of the mind are the same as those muscles. The higher plane that you've discovered may not be the summit. You may need a Divine instructor to nudge your thoughts to the next plateau.
- **I can have everything.** All of your needs are

supplied. Already. Period. All that God is, all that He's made, is mine to claim and allow entry into my world through my relationships with others.

- **Success will come through love and health.** Success is taking one positive action—nothing more. When you love others and yourself, when your body and thoughts are healthy, you can take those positive actions moment by moment, day by day.

- **It will be for all to share; if not to give, what good is wealth?** Because you know that you only have what you give, your successes are secured when you share them. If you continue to give and eventually begin to "run on empty," you can become resentful. It's imperative that you take care of yourself so you can give yourself to others.

- **Watching lives make changes because of words I've spoken.** Seeing with your own eyes the choices and changes others make because of a conversation you've had encourages your own growth and belief that all things are possible. It's not what you might have said that made a difference, but what they heard and took action on that has made all the difference.

- **Hopeful rearranges for hearts that once were broken.** Sometimes the rearranges are painful endings to relationships, moves to new locations, letting go of children and their lives, or living in the empty nest. Just think, it could be the "empty next!" Yet there's hope in the present moment. The pain ceases when you "out frame," or step away from the center of the pain of the moment, and say, "This is the best thing that could've ever happened."

- **What I have I want to share.** What you share, you have. So in order to continue your "work in progress," you must share.
- **You'll never know, want, or need.** Your wants for material things dissolve into one major desire: To be there for others. Then your needs will always be met because they're always brought through others.
- **I can have everything with faith as big as one small seed.** Think of the parable of the mustard seed, so remarkably small that you can barely hold it between your finger and thumb. Yet the promise is that if you believe with as much faith as the size of that tiny seed, you can do and you can have everything. The message here is focused belief.
- **I can do, you can too, everything: We'll have everything with faith as big as one small seed.** It's for us all today. You. Me. Everyone in our path. We have but one responsibility and that's to shine as the stars that we are, to share the message of faith with others.

Think It, Be It

So if you can do anything, can you also do everything? Can you be everything? No, and no. The better question is, what can you be? You can be everything that *you* can be. To define what that is is to define your values, the gifts that you've been given and used effectively, the usefulness of your body, and your thought processes. You can be fully everything that you are designed to be, and what you most need to do is to focus on being that and that alone.

To tell the whole truth, I've always wanted to be an actress. From the days of watching the glamorous Loretta Young emerge from the doorway of her apartment on the set of her 1950s television show, to Dale Evans riding confidently on Buttermilk to her home on the Double R Ranch, there has been a draw for me to be just like them. I confess: I've wanted to have the camera, the spotlight, to be recognized, and remembered.

The denial of this girlhood dream began when my family would leave my grandparent's home, which we referred to as "down home," and drive back to Ohio and the parsonage. When we arrived at the crest of the hill, there'd always be a movie playing at the Woodlawn Drive-In. It would flicker in the night sky, in black and white, and we could easily see it from the road. We were tiny, my sisters and I, and mother would always say, "Turn your heads, girls; those are naughty pictures."

The idea of being an actress in "naughty pictures" was outside the realm of the church and my saintly parents. So early on I learned to stuff my dream away. It would come out camouflaged in other activities; acting in the junior class play *Don't Take My Penny*, where I was Mavis, a radio personality; winning Greene County's Junior Miss Pageant crown and going into the Ohio pageant; then being active in college drama (*Our Miss Brooks*) and community theater post-college (*The Tender Trap* and *You Can't Take It with You*).

My work with REDKEN was a place where I could use my acting skills in front of live audiences and video cameras, on a platform stage, and in the spotlight. I was the actress I always dreamed of being in a safe and secure position, contributing to the lives of salon professionals through worldwide educational events. My acting dream has served REDKEN, the industry, and my family very well for thirty years.

Not long after my move to Los Angeles, I auditioned for an actors' workshop group where I could create a spot to study my craft. I wasn't seriously thinking of film acting, but I believed that studying with those whose lives were dedicated to making it in television, film, and commercials would be a good experience for me. And the workshops did enhance my memory, speaking, and training skills.

I recall the day I read for my audition and discovered that I had secured a place in the next class. The group met on Tuesday and Thursday nights. It took commitment from me to rearrange my already hectic travel schedule. I was up to the challenge. I wanted to do this.

Sauntering to my car, the same 1973 Cutlass that carried me across the country to the west coast, I took a look at my reflection in the rearview mirror. I felt I had scored a major goal and was taking a giant step toward my secret dream. As I drove away, I felt the urge to write the following poem.

I'm on My Way to Becoming

I'm on my way to becoming
Everything that I can be
I'm on my way to discovering
Everything inside of me
My fears are gone
My thoughts are on
The person that hides within me

I'm becoming
I'm becoming
I am becoming

- **I'm on my way to becoming everything that I can be.** This is the key to life. Everyday is one more opportunity to take the next positive step toward being the kind of person you desire to become. I remind you again of the words written on the windows at Saks Fifth Avenue: "Work in Progress." Let those words remind you of your own life, to stay in the present realizing that you, too, are a work in progress on your way to becoming.

- **I'm on my way to discovering everything inside of me.** Again, the call goes deep within. It asks that you stay on the discovery path and be willing to open those closed spaces within that you've keep secret all your life. It asks that you open them up and see that everything can contribute to the highest vision of who you are and thus how you see the world. What's inside besides healthy functioning organs, muscles, tissues, and cells? The other inner life that you'll discover is your conscience, value system, your drive and need, and your desire and gratitude.

- **My fears are gone.** Now, this is *big*. Can you really say this with radical honesty? Will you never have a moment when that ugly demon strikes in the pit of your stomach or makes your palms sweat? Will you never again experience the sputtering of your heart or the stammering of your tongue in one of those "five-year-old" unsure moments? The answer is "yes"—yes you will. Again and again. Behind the drama, there is peace and serenity, and the fear is not only gone—it doesn't exist. How can you be sure of this? When you look at everything that is happening through the eyes of divine Love, the result can only be love. Love and fear are incompatible and cannot occupy the same space at the same time. One has to go. Remember, if you find love in the situation, fear departs. Remind yourself, "This is the best thing that could've ever happened," and embrace it as the truth.

- **My thoughts are on the person that hides within me.** The actress in me has been hiding since my earliest remembrances. There may be one who hides within you who is aching to come out and make him or herself known. Like my story, you may find alternative ways of satisfying that desire through meaningful and purposeful expression. It may not be as literal as it may seem, however. The freedom to recognize who that person is, give it a life, and be proud of who it is will open opportunities to live with your truth like you've never done before. You may see changes in your body, your friends, and your habits in order to support the lifestyle and image that this person prefers.

Keep your thoughts on allowing expression of your hidden person. Opportunities for continued expression will be poured onto your path, until you fully be the *star right where you are!*

epilogue

I find it amazing that I've become such a New Yorker, and I feel that my city has been violated beyond belief. I would never have dreamed in a million years that I'd live in New York and have a love affair with it. Every time I fill out an application and print my address on 49th Street in New York, I take a deep breath and reach out to someone around me to ask, "Would you pinch me?" just to make sure I'm not making this up.

In the past I traveled to New York City on business trips, normally once a year for the huge International Beauty Show at the Javits Center. After about three days, my skin would begin to crawl and I'd say under my breath, "Get me out of here!" California's sunny days and palm trees were always a welcome sight when I'd return home.

After REDKEN's acquisition by L'Oreal USA in June 1994, it was understood that we would continue our operation on the West Coast. We'd have all L'Oreal's resources in New York. All was well.

On Sunday night, January 16, I was sitting in the safety of my new condominium that I'd just moved into and finished decorating over the Christmas holidays. My parents had traveled to Los Angeles to celebrate with me, and my dad helped me build a wall of bookshelves in the living room to house my friends—my books—and the treasures I'd collected from around the world.

Sipping tea, watching the fire in the fireplace, listening to smooth jazz on my sound system, I was so grateful and found myself thanking God out loud for my beautiful safe harbor.

At around 11 P.M., I prepared my home for the night, made my way up the stairs to my master bedroom, and fell into a gentle sleep.

At four-thirty in the morning, I was shot from my bed. The whole house was swinging, shaking. I made my way over to the doorjamb and stood there listening to my house breaking apart downstairs.

I knew what it was . . . the "Big One" we'd been waiting for. Without thought, I began singing at the top of my lungs an old hymn of the church:

> "On Christ the solid rock I stand
> All other ground is sinking sand
> All other ground is sinking sand."

Finally, after forty-eight seconds, the movement stopped. I put on clothes and my shoes, and made my way outside to the parking lot where I huddled with my neighbors. The pastor of a small Church of the Nazarene walked across the street and offered us to come to safety provided by the strength of his A-frame sanctuary. There, we were served coffee and donuts and blankets to stay warm in the early hours of a wintry California morning.

When the sun began to break, I walked through the church and saw a telephone. Never dreaming there would be a clear line, I jokingly picked it up . . . and *voila*: There was a dial tone!

My parents—always my first point of contact—had been watching *Good Morning America* and saw the destruction. How relieved they were to know I was all right. I remember speaking through my tears something about learning the lesson of "just things" and would call them again soon to keep them informed of what I discovered when I reentered my home.

It was shocking. The peaceful place of just a few hours before was now in shambles. The bookcases and fireplace had fallen, the glass top tables were broken, the kitchen cabinets and refrigerator were jarred open, and glass and food were everywhere.

I slowly made my way through the rubble with yet another song running through my head.

"Where the Spirit of the Lord is, there is peace
Where the Spirit of the Lord is, there is hope.
There is comfort in life's darkest hour
There is light and help there is peace and power
In the Spirit, in the Spirit of the Lord."

Over and over it played in my head as I tried to think of where to begin the cleanup process. I made my way upstairs to my bedroom and bath: same scene. And water everywhere. I pulled the shower curtain back, and there were my REDKEN products. They must have moved with every jolt until they stopped, huddled together at the drain. When I looked at them, my imagination heard them say, "Don't worry, Annie; we're still here."

I smiled.

In the ensuing months, we repaired our company, our home, and our lives. We were only five miles from the epicenter of the 6.8 quake and had a real jolt. The biggest aftershock was to come within a few weeks.

It was announced that REDKEN would move to New York City, the headquarters of L'Oreal USA.

New York! Oh no, not New York! I thought to myself. There was nowhere else on the planet that I wanted to live in less than New York. Ugly and loud, rude and big, boisterous and dirty New York. Say it isn't so!

But it was so. And when all was said and done, thirty-three of us, out of 300 employees, said, "We'll go." By August 1994, we were "New Yorkas."

My decision to go wasn't that easy. It wasn't a done deal right off the bat. It wasn't until Easter Sunday evening that I had an affirmation that I needed to move.

I sat at my pool on Easter afternoon, sunshine warming my body and melting my thoughts. In about an hour, my normal sunning time, I "heard" the Lord say, "Go into your house and watch *Beauty and the Beast*": My favorite animated film of all time.

So I obeyed. I popped a big bowl of popcorn, sat in front of my TV, pushed "play," and began watching the story of Belle and the ugly, loud, rude, big and boisterous, dirty Beast. I watched the story closely, looking for the message I was drawn to receive.

I began to relate to Belle—frail, scared, and threatened

(acquisition, earthquake, move)—and there was the Beast: New York. Oh my goodness, it was the same! And I kept watching. Something began to happen to Belle as she was around the Beast more and more. She saw redeeming qualities: playfulness, compassion, and generosity. But it wasn't until she was the first to say, "I love you," that the Beast transformed.

There it was! My answer whether to go or not. I changed my perspective of New York and decided to be the first to say, "I love you, New York," and when I arrived I saw the beauty, playfulness, compassion, and generosity of New Yorkers. It was going to be just fine.

And it has been just fine. So now, twelve years later, I find myself defending the redeeming qualities of my home and wanting to do whatever I can to restore the hopes and dreams of New York and New Yorkers, of America and Americans. I know it will be through demonstrating Love in all that I think, say, and do—because, yes, it bears saying again, Love and Fear cannot dwell in the same space at the same time.

I choose Love. I choose to serve. I choose to glow as the star that I am. Will you join me?

You will find, as I have, the more you are authentically you, the more you are trusted. Others will sense how congruent you are, all Five GLOWpoints aligned. What they're drawn to is not you so much as it is their own glow—their own faith—through what they sense in you.

This is the happily ever after.

Here's what I want you to do. Take a long look at the star field on the American flag (or, if you're from a country where you have a star on your flag, you can use your flag) and claim one of those stars as your very own. Every time you see the flag from now on, reaffirm your place as that star by saying, "That's me!" Commit to the healthy awareness of the Five GLOWpoints we've covered in this book.

It is my conviction that America will stay beautiful as Americans stay beautiful and healthy, positive, and financially sound, and as they serve from a heart of love. We are blessed to be in a country where we have the freedom to be beautiful. As we've seen the pictures of women covered from head to toe and then compare those images with women I see on the streets of New York everyday—carrying computer cases, listening to music on their iPODs, catching a bus ride, hailing a taxi, and wearing whatever they want to wear—I give thanks for a country where we have the freedom to "be you to full."

I give thanks for living in a country where we have the freedom to create beauty. The people in the industry I serve dedicate themselves to this as they turn the key to their salons everyday. And I give thanks for living in a country where I've had the freedom to encourage others to learn the best techniques and technologies, to earn the highest income, and to live the best lives they can dream of. I'm thankful that my company, REDKEN, has dedicated its mission for four decades to this quest.

As we celebrate these freedoms, let's dedicate ourselves to them in honor of those who no longer have the opportunity to enjoy the pursuit of beauty.

I was invited to spend a few moments one evening with a visiting Japanese priest who was taking private sessions with individuals in fifteen-minute segments. I made an appointment, showing up ten minutes ahead of my appointment time. After waiting a few minutes, a young Japanese boy came to escort me into a counseling room. He asked if I had three issues that I wanted to discuss with the monk relating to health, job, family, or relationship. I thought for a moment, and then responded. "I don't think I have three issues. But, if I did, they would be one, I want to know I'm living from my authentic energy; two, I want my body to reflect that authentic energy and need to know how to feed it, rest, and exercise it; and three, I want to speak with boldness from that authentic energy." The boy wrote the three issues in Japanese on a card and thanked me—after looking at me strangely and admitting that these were different requests than what they normally hear.

The boy escorted me back to the living room. Shortly a Japanese girl came to take me in to see him. Dressed in traditional robes, with a slick-bald head and small wire-rimmed glasses, he sat on a chair in the corner of the room.

I sat in front of him on the floor, comfortable on a pillow. The girl took her place to my left. She handed him my card. He looked at it, read it thoroughly, and began laughing, his voice resonating and filling the entire room with its richness.

My little Annie once again rose to the occasion: "Oh no, I'm so stupid. What did I say that was so funny? How is he going to respond to me?"

Then he spoke, and through the young girl came the translation.

"What are you afraid of?"

I actually began to answer him with the first word that came to my mind: "Power." But before I could speak, he continued.

"You were born with this. Believe God 100 percent and that is all."

Looking at the girl, I said, "That's all?" And she nodded. I asked if I could touch him and just as I said it, he reached out his hands and I placed each one on the sides of my face. I gave her a hug. I left the room.

Some people felt healed following their session. Some felt definite energy shifts. I felt nothing. Just a nice experience that I probably wouldn't have again. But I couldn't get his words out of my mind and heart. "Believe God 100 percent and that is all."

Beginning today, let's balance each of our Five GLOW points—body, thoughts, relationships, resources, and service—so we live in the place that reflects the truth, "You Are A Star Right Where You Are."

Let's believe Him 100 percent.

And that is all.

Thirty years in the professional salon industry have given me pause to ask myself the same questions I've been asked by others: What's kept me going? Why, as a nonhairdresser, would I devote my life to this industry? How do I continue to serve whomever, whenever, and wherever the invitation is extended? Why have I done this work to the sacrifice of having a "regular" life with a significant other, family, and home?

The scriptures implore us to be able to give a reason for the hope that is within us, to be able to explain why we are blessed beyond measure, to thank that One who created us and created the places for us to serve. I trust that this book answered those questions once and for all, and has offered the practices that have become my lifeline.

God grant me the serenity to accept the things I cannot change
God grant me the courage to change the things I can
And grant me the wisdom to know what the difference is
So I can live my life, safely, in your will today.

about the author

In 2005, Ann Mincey celebrates her thirtieth year with REDKEN 5th Avenue NYC. Her leadership in the professional salon industry has been extraordinary, and her contributions are countless.

Serving salon professionals all over the world, Ann has shared her inspiration by speaking and training on all the major continents.

Ann has attained remarkable measures in conveying the message of the professional salon industry to the consumer public through her contribution to REDKEN's public relations in leading beauty/fashion and trade press. She also serves on the faculty as director of health, beauty and spirit for Shape Your Life destination resort programs.

In 1999, as part of Southern Nazarene University's centennial celebration, Ann was named as one of 100 alumni for outstanding impact of business in the world. She was named—along with fellow classmates Brad Moore, president of Hallmark Productions; and Boyd Matson, former host of *National Geographic Explorer*—as outstanding alumna in the Coalition of Christian Colleges and Universities.

During 2002, Ann was invited to speak at the Women's Peace Initiative in Geneva, Switzerland, on the topic of "The Beauty of Peace and the Peace of Beauty."

Ann received the Star Award given by the New York Women's Agenda, a group of 100 women's organizations representing 100,000 businesswomen in New York City, for her contribution to her community, her industry, and the world of business.

She was instrumental in raising over $570,000 for the American Heart Association as chairperson of the American Beauty Association Beauty Ball.

Ann was inducted into the North American Hairstyling Awards Hall of Leaders in January 2003. The award was presented on behalf of her dedication each day to REDKEN and to encouraging salon professionals to "earn a better living and live a better life."

The National Professional Beauty Industry Council and the City of Hope Cancer Research and Treatment Center named Ann the Spirit of Life honoree for 2004. Her goal of raising a million dollars for ongoing research for breast cancer was exceeded as she presented a check of $1,400,000 to the City of Hope, a leading research and treatment center for life-threatening diseases. The intention to accept the honor came out of her desire to honor her sister, Cathy Lynn; REDKEN colleagues; and thousands of women from the salon community who have been diagnosed with breast cancer.

In 2004, Ann was named to the National Cosmetology Association Hall of Renown.

music references

"I'll Be a Sunbeam"
Words: Nellie Talbot
Music: Edwin O. Excell

"On a Clear Day"
Words: Alan Jay Lerner
Music: Burton Lane

"America the Beautiful"
Words: Katharine Lee Bates
Music: Samuel A. Ward

"Blue Skies"
Words and music: Irving Berlin

"Oh Love That Will Not Let Me Go"
Words: George Matheson 1882
Music: Albert L. Peace 1884

"I Don't Have to Wait until I'm Grown Up"
author unknown

"Where the Spirit of the Lord Is"
Words and music: Stephen R. Adams

"The Solid Rock"
Words: Edward Nate
Music: William B. Bradbury

"Quiet Moments with God"
Lloyd John Ogilvie
Copyright 2000 by Harvest House Publishers
Eugene, Oregon